CHOOSE YOUR WEAPONS—
AND YOUR TARGETS

You can turn computers, clocks, answering machines, pocket calculators, sheets of plastic wrap, and all the other conveniences of modern living into the latest, greatest weapons of wickedly funny wit.

You can make your friends, your brothers and sisters, your spouse, your boss, the squirming sources of your not-so-innocent merriment.

In this book you will find scores of thoroughly up-to-date ways to make today's world a little brighter (and a lot crazier). But act fast—before someone beats you to it!

THE SECOND OFFICIAL
HANDBOOK
OF PRACTICAL
JOKES

The Illustrated Book of Nude Photography

Complete with a special appendix on the appendix.

Charles Windsor

The Big Book of Difficult Equations, and Yam Recipes

includes exponentials, tangential arcs, and sweet potato gravy

Peter van der Linden

The Second Official
Handbook
of Practical
Jokes

The misappliance of science
with a gross of other Practical Jokes, Pranks, Jests,
Tricks, Stunts, Ruses, Gags, Antics,
Larks, Capers, Hoaxes, Frolics, etc.

Peter van der Linden

Illustrated by Michael Salter

A SIGNET BOOK

SIGNET
Published by the Penguin Group
Penguin Books USA Inc., 375 Hudson Street,
New York, New York 10014, U.S.A.
Penguin Books Ltd, 27 Wrights Lane,
London W8 5TZ, England
Penguin Books Australia Ltd, Ringwood,
Victoria, Australia
Penguin Books Canada Ltd, 2801 John Street,
Markham, Ontario, Canada L3R 1B4
Penguin Books (N.Z.) Ltd, 182-190 Wairau Road,
Auckland 10, New Zealand

Penguin Books Ltd, Registered Offices:
Harmondsworth, Middlesex, England

First published by Signet, an imprint of New American Library, a
division of Penguin Books USA Inc.

First Printing, March, 1991
10 9 8 7 6 5 4 3 2 1

Copyright © Peter van der Linden, 1991
All rights reserved

 REGISTERED TRADEMARK—MARCA REGISTRADA

Printed in the United States of America

This book is intended for entertainment and humor purposes only. Neither
the author nor the publisher can assume any responsibility for the use or misuse
of any information contained within this book.

The Captain and the Kangaroo—Dedication

In 1770 the explorer Captain James Cook landed on the east coast of Australia, seeking haven from a series of tropical storms. Cook spent three months inside the Great Barrier Reef—in those days, of course, it was merely an okay barrier reef—while his ship was repaired and reprovisioned, and he befriended the native aborigines. Cook picked up a smattering of the Bushmen's language and used this to learn about the strange Australian plants and animals.

One day, Cook pointed to a kangaroo, and asked in the native dialect, "What is the name of that strange animal that bounces from place to place?" A Bushman looked over to where Cook was pointing and replied "kangaroo." Ever since, the hopping furry beast has been known by that name. However, "kangaroo" does not mean "hopping furry beast that bounces from place to place." "Kangaroo" is actually the Bushman phrase meaning, "Pardon, what did you say?"

Cook was later clubbed to death in Hawaii by natives whom he mistakenly believed were seeking to worship him as a god. His failure to rise again on the third day merely confirmed their suspicions. This book is therefore dedicated to Captain James Cook, in recognition of his astounding ability to misunderstand just about anything.

Pvd L.

Acknowledgments

Many thanks to all my friends who generously played their best practical jokes on me, and then let me write about it. Special thanks to Lawrie Webb, to Nick Corder, and to the bottle of thirty-five-year-old malt scotch that they put away last time I had them both at my house together. Some of their suggestions really illustrate the problems of trying to combine a scotch-tasting with a joke-planning session.

Thanks, too, to Frank Reid who constantly amazes me with his talents and ingenuity.

I must also give due credit to my dear friend Furball. I neglected to acknowledge her in *The Official Handbook of Practical Jokes*, and her hit-men have been shadowing me ever since. She is creative, bright, totally vicious about grammar, and can work wonders with a microwave.

Last and least, to Dirk Wibble O'Dooley who I promised to mention in this book: Hi there, big fella!

Contents

This book contains only the finest figures, rudiments, grammar, syntax, poetry, and rhetoric. We hope that this book reaches you in the very best of condition, and that you enjoy sampling its pages.

The humor contained in this book may be indigestible if swallowed whole. Certain wisecracks may cause shortness of breath, labored breathing, runny eyes, or aching sides. If for any reason, an adverse reaction occurs with this or any book, please wash out the eyes thoroughly with warm water, and discontinue use of the product.

Foreword by Pope John-Paul III

As both my father and my grandfather before me discovered, having the first name "Pope" combined with our unusual family surname of "John-Paul" has opened many doors. One portal that I would have preferred remained permanently shut however was the door over which the author of this book had suspended a bucket of ice water back when we were in school together. He certainly served me up a doozie that time, claiming afterward that the whole thing was an error on my part and that I had ruined his thermodynamics project experiment. Of course, the author is no Jack Kennedy, as any of his ex-wives or numerous paramours will attest. And in all fairness, he's no Dan Quayle either. But enough of the author, let's talk about the book.

Every once in a while a book comes along that is so original, so entertaining, so refreshing that it captures the public imagination, and shoots straight to the top of the *New York Times* best-seller list, staying there for over a year and generating millions in residuals. Friends—this is probably not such a book. But you never know for sure, and why risk being the victim of a practical joke instead of the guffawing protagonist?

Sour-faced critics will always complain that practical jokes are about as useful as a chocolate teapot, but that misses the point. This book will galvanize the jaded mind, and rejuvenate even the most tired spirit. At the very least it can be employed as a flyswatter or, if printed on softer paper, could perhaps be of some use in the bathroom.

In conclusion, therefore, let me advise in the words of the John-Paul family motto, *"De rerum novarum et spiritu tutti frutti lux et vino veritas"* (or in English, "drink new wine, it's light and very tasty").

Pope John-Paul III, Rome, NY

"And unextinguishable laughter rose among the gods"
—Homer, *Iliad*, Bk i, 1. 599.

Introduction
Go West,
Young Pest

It's not easy being a practical joker. People have *expectations* of you. They expect you to come from California, for one thing. Like the San Andreas fault, radical surprises seem to run through the heart of the West Coast, and I wanted in. From my earliest days therefore, I was westward-bound seeking a blend of California, karma, and comedy. It's a tough break on a kid to be born within earshot of Bow Bells, London (and thus technically be a Cockney), yet know instinctively that his spiritual home is with the Californians, not the costermongers. But I knew I had to leave home ever since the unfortunate incident involving the denture adhesive I spread over the toilet seat when I was three years old.

Though the firemen eventually freed Dad (they said they used the solvent "assetone"), it was a long while before he smiled again—mostly because with denture adhesive now banned from the house, his teeth were always falling out.

The world has an attitude about California; people think that the state is a wacky, eccentric place, overflowing with colorful characters who snack on granola bars and tofu while roller-skating to the beach. Whoa dudes! That's no spiff riff! Many Californians can't stand the high-cholesterol taste of tofu; the rest of it is all true though.

They say that California is a state of mind. The first hippies came from San Francisco, and the last ones can still be seen there,* some in the zoo, and some free-range ones roaming the streets of Haight-Ashbury in their colorful tie-dyed plumage. Lottery rules from other

* Some zoologists claim to have sighted hippie tribes in Hawaii, validating the theory that simplistic life forms such as coconuts, reeds, lizards, or followers of the Grateful Dead can be blown great distances across the ocean clinging to debris, and eventually mate and establish new colonies.

states and the fine print of product warranties often specify "does not apply in California." Indeed, this is true for much of life's conventional wisdom. It simply does not apply in California. In short, I knew from an early age that the Golden State was the one for me.

But where in California? The left coast can be an awkward place seismically. With every earthquake the streets spontaneously rearrange themselves. Obviously I wanted to live in an area where the people had more culture than the average Petri dish, and where practical joking was accepted as an art form. I first moved to San Francisco, but after a few months (and several spectacular capers) the authorities convinced me my niche lay elsewhere. The natives were friendly enough, but a certain *je-ne-sais-quoi* was missing, and I didn't know what it was. A trusted friend confided that real cool was in Southern California, and within a week I decamped to Los Angeles. People leaving San Francisco often refer to it as "de-camping" for some reason.

The City of The Angels, for those who don't know, is a vast sprawling mass stretching from Beverly Hills in the north to Long Beach in the south, and out to Pasadena (home of the "little old lady" of automotive song fame) in the east. Shunning the gaudy ostentation of Hollywood's multimillion dollar homes, I settled in the more modest suburb of Watts. Several weeks went by, and the most eccentric thing I encountered was the appearance of triple-strength peppers on my pizza. I ate several such meals before realizing that my error lay in not tipping the delivery boy. Clearly I had missed the epicenter of cool.

The neighbors soon put me right. "You want Venice Beach," they said, adding helpfully, "that's where all the real weirdos hang out." Whether they were genuinely trying to assist me, or merely encouraging me to move on, I never discovered, but nonetheless I relocated at once to the seashore. As Sherlock Holmes once remarked, "the game's a hotfoot," and once on the trail, I was not to be easily thrown off. Venice Beach was certainly closer to the freewheeling ideology that I sought, but I hadn't yet found the hub.

The next few weeks were a blur as I followed successively more specific advice: "Try Ocean Front Walk," "Other end! Up by 18th and 19th." "Not this building! That one!" "Top floor apartment." At last I had homed in on the source of California cool! I entered the top floor apartment, pretending to be a short-term roommate. The other roomies were all heavyset individuals with long lank hair and muscular tattooed forearms like Popeye's. They looked like ex-professional wrestlers who had gone to seed after the only thing they could throw was a fight. They looked like someone should lock them up in a room and throw away the room.

Yes, they were an ugly bunch of women, and they sized me up right away. "Check out the bathroom," they confided, so I went in to take a shower. It looked good. In LA things always look better than they are. I spun the chromed lever marked "hot," and a jet of ice cold water spat right out of the nozzle into my face. The lever came off in my hand, which was now coated with wet silver paint. I went to the washbasin to rinse it off, and discovered—too late—that the U-bend had been removed from the sink, and the open pipe discharged straight onto my knees. It was the kind of place where I felt immediately at home. If you can't take it you shouldn't dish it out. I *told* you it's not easy being a practical joker.

The Twelve Basic Jokes

Everyone has heard the folklore that there are only twelve basic jokes, and all witticisms are variants of one of these elementary forms. It seems impossible to find anything describing exactly what these twelve jokes are, however. As a public service, therefore, I plan to list all of them in *The Third Official Handbook of Practical Jokes*.

It is possible to categorize humor in several other ways. In The Official Handbook of Practical Jokes I described the Boomerang (a joke that backfires) and the Zinger (a double joke). We can also classify jokes into one of three basic categories. The three classes blend into each other at their boundaries, and every leg-pull ever played falls into one of these groups. In order of sophistication, simplest first, we have:

Class 1 Practical Joke—the simplest of tricks, giving a result that is surprising to somebody, and amusing to everyone else. Effects such as unscrewing the salt shaker lid, or turning on the sprinkler at a lawn party are class 1 pranks. At the low end they too easily degenerate into simple harassment. Guard against this! The humor comes in selecting the right victim and the right effect. Class 1 jokes are great for helping haughty people get some fun in life.

Class 2 Practical Joke—a more refined version of class 1, tricks in this category do not take place at anybody's expense. They simply provide a surprising and amusing effect. My good friend Harris once put up a sign in an open field otherwise untouched by human presence, reading, DO NOT THROW STONES AT THIS SIGN. Like judo, a class 2 joke lures the participant into overcoming himself, only it uses the mind rather than body weight. The confusion factor figures large in class 2.

Class 3 Practical Joke—these are hoaxes where the laws of nature are apparently broken, or at least severely stretched. A class 3 prank confronts the victim with an unusual circumstance and often lures him into believing a totally ridiculous explanation for it.

Class 3 tricks can be simple—plane your dad's builder's level ("Gee, I just can't understand why everything I build comes out crooked now . . .) —or elaborate. In the first Handbook I explained the old chestnut of Saran-wrapping a toilet. Kid's stuff! Used creatively, Saran Wrap can create "invisible force fields" to bend many a fine brain. Tape some strips across a door frame from chest to knee height, making sure not to leave any wrinkles. Leave part of the frame uncovered so there's no suction when the door is opened. I need not explain what happens to a person accidentally walking into an invisible wall. For best results, try it in a poorly lighted establishment or the morning after a really good party.

In addition, a joker gains credit in proportion to the number of people he takes in, and for the scale of the enterprise. Selling London Bridge to one person is pretty good; persuading the entire council of Lake Havasu City to buy it and ship it out to the Arizona desert is a masterstroke.

I like subtlety in a practical joke. It can be immensely funnier when the patsy does not realize he has been set up. Plus you have the advantage that you do not inspire revenge. Strive for finesse, delicate effects, and don't tell 'em when you're fooling!

Defenses

You don't have to be a fall guy when a victim accuses you of setting him up, and seeks revenge. Try applying any of the following defenses. If they are good enough for our top politicians, they are good enough for you.

> The "'Nixon Defense"—lie through your teeth, and destroy the evidence.

> The "Gerald Ford Defense"—essentially a sympathy bid, trip over your own feet, fall down, invite them to a round of golf.

> The "Reagan Memory Lapse"—grin like a loon, and tell them you have "no recollection" of the incident, and that your heart and best intentions tell you it never happened.

> The "Quayle Excuse"—there is no excuse for J. Danforth Quayle, III.

If none of these work, blame anyone who isn't there. A marginal ploy, like suddenly confessing to being your evil twin brother who is playing a trick on both of you, is a sure sign of desperation.

Pay Attention to these Serious Warnings

Practical jokes must always be harmless and easily reversible, otherwise the prankster has strayed over the boundary into nuisance, which is not funny. Never do anything that is illegal or that might be dangerous. Never do anything that might injure or hurt someone. The victim of a practical joke should be an extroverted person, capable of withstanding mild fun-poking. Generally, the more self-assured the victim, the more hilarious it is to see him struggle with the outcome of some bizarre gag. And remember kids, Batman doesn't really fly.

New
Classic Fun

"Classics are the noblest recorded thoughts of Man"
HENRY DAVID THOREAU

You don't have to spend much time practical joking before you build up a large collection of classic tricks. All the practical jokes in this chapter have a special place in my heart. It's right on the aorta, up by the left ventricle. There's always a proper time and place for practical joking, and that's especially appropriate since many of the tricks in this chapter deal with the masterful manipulation of either time or place.

Pranksters are opportunists, cleverly taking advantage of any situation to turn it into something strange. I'll never forget the time I went backpacking with Harris. All the pots and pans were strapped on the outside of my pack. As I led the way along the trail, I gradually felt that my pack was getting heavier and heavier. A lunchtime stop confirmed why. Harris had been filling my pans with rocks as we went along. I dunked his fat head in the stream, and then secretly filled his pepper pot with specks of dirt. When he complained that the pepper was stale, I told him "Well, use more—in fact use lots of it." That night, after I had settled down in the tent, Harris filled my boots with cold soup. We were awakened in the middle of the night by a band of weasels attacking my footwear. We beat them off, and recovered the boots, but for the rest of the trip I could not keep flies and small animals away from my feet. Bright eyes lined the bushes by the side of the trail, as the weasels, polecats, stoats, and ferrets waited for me to drop my vigilance, so they could again run off with the booty.

The confusion resulting from practical jokes is actually a valuable lesson: Life is more than just an ordered progression between planned events, and some

times creativity, spontaneity, and depravity have a place. Just don't expect your victims to thank you for it.

1

A "glitter trap" is only a simple class 1 practical joke, but it has the special feature that the victim causes his own demise. If you were marooned on a desert isle and could only take one practical joke with you, this should be the one. Glitter traps are popular in offices and computer rooms with high false ceilings. One of the ceiling tiles over the victim's head is rigged so that it can fall open, allowing a pile of silver glitter Christmas decoration on top to stream downward.

The trapdoor ceiling tile is lightly pinned shut, and a concealed string run from the pin, inside the ceiling, down the wall, to the back of a drawer in the victim's desk. When the drawer is opened, the string is pulled, the pin jerked free, causing an instant indoor blizzard!

2

Barry Nordin, who lives in Rhode Island, has been pulling off imaginative jokes for many years. Some classic fooling happened at his place of work, when the popular company president was transferred abroad. The staff held a testimonial dinner, which Barry turned into a real roasting. As each speaker finished, he or she would present the president with a small gift. When Barry's turn came, he and his accomplice staged a double act of ten minutes of comedy, in which they saved the best gag for last.

Barry concluded his toast by announcing, "We searched high and low for a really worthwhile gift, and we finally found a rare crystal goblet made by Paul Revere. As you know, Revere made his name as a silversmith, but he did create a small collection of handblown glass chalices. These pieces are of astonishing beauty, and are literally irreplaceable. We are pleased to present you, as a mark of our esteem, with one of these delicate goblets."

Gesturing for his accomplice to give him the handsomely wrapped box, Barry reached for it but stumbled, and the box fell through his hands. It hit the floor with an ear-shattering sound of smashing glass that shocked the 200 guests into numbed silence. Barry and his accomplice exchanged forlorn glances, turned to the president, said "Never mind" in unison, and walked back to their seats, leaving the box where it fell. Everyone became hysterical. Of course, the box contained only shards of previously broken glass held at one end by tissue paper that parted when it hit the floor.

3

One of my best-loved stories concerns a practical joke played, not by me, but by Mother Nature. Needless to say, I got the blame for it anyway. It all started when my very good friend Harris came to visit me in California. Harris and I go back a long way, back to the days when I pulled him through college. Through my careful shepherding, and despite the dire predictions of all his professors, I was able to get him to graduate. He's like a brother to me, except his ears stick out more.

Harris landed at San Francisco airport, where I met him and drove us home. By chance, a few hours after he arrived a small earthquake struck (a fairly common event) and gently vibrated the house. At the exact moment the tremor struck, Harris was sitting on the can in the bathroom. The resultant sweeping action of the water sloshing back and forward in the can deluded him into thinking that he was sitting on a bidet. He actually formed the impression that I was sassing him by remotely activating the plumbing! How he could have got this opinion of me I just don't know.

Harris bailed out and came running furiously through the house, his pants flapping around his ankles, hot on the warpath. He caught up with me in the garden where I was showing my begonias to a retired ladies gardening club. Harris and the ladies made quite an impression on each other. In fact I haven't seen so much emotion on Harris's face since the time he went long on blue chips and the next day the stock market fell 508 points. I told him later that we didn't have a bidet, and that we had actually experienced a mild earthquake.

Even though Harris always pans this story and asks me to "can" it, I am flushed with success because it is one of the few times I have bested him in a practical joke. And I didn't even do anything to incommode him.

4

Harris never forgot his awful experience, and quite unjustly he never forgave me either. He lives in Hong Kong now, where he is an investment banker, and employs hundreds of native Chinese who carry out his daily bidding while he regally oversees activities from the golf course.

I went out to visit Harris for a vacation, and when he met me I noted that he had grown a small mustache since I last saw him. "Oh this?" Harris explained. "It's a fake mustache actually." Seeing my look of disbelief, he peeled it back a little. It *was* a fake mustache, and he told me that the Chinese have great difficulty in growing facial hair. According to Harris, anyone in Hong Kong who has a mustache or beard is held in high esteem. Facial hair is a status symbol, he said, that confers great authority on the wearer. He therefore wears the faux mustache whenever he is out of the house.

I was somewhat skeptical until Harris staged a demonstration. At the next street corner he purchased a newspaper, and the vendor fawned all over him, treating Harris like a young god. We continued down the street, Harris removed his adornment, and repeated the paper purchase with a different vendor. This time the newsboy treated us with indifference.

With the thoughtfulness typical of a kind friend, Harris mentioned that he had been able to procure similarly-realistic false whiskers for me. He produced a frighteningly large handlebar mustache and proceeded to gum it to my upper lip. The effect was similar to wearing a small Scottish terrier on my face. Harris stressed the importance of not letting any of his household staff see me without my new disguise, for fear that we should both lose face.

And so it was for the whole three weeks I spent with Harris in the tropical humidity, we went everywhere wearing our false whiskers—Harris with a small trim mustache, and me weighed down with a gigantic furry handlebar. To this day, I have not been able to decide how much, if any, of Harris's story is true. My pride does not permit me to inquire too closely into the matter.

5

Plant a set of instructions for a symphony orchestra conductor. When he walks out to the podium and inspects the music, he should find a small neatly lettered note reading:

Wave your hands until the music stops.
Then take a bow.

6

In any other place my colleague "Nerdy" Bob Byteswap would come in for a lot of abuse. He's a slightly-built guy who always wears wire-framed glasses with fish-tank lenses, sort of like John Denver with brains. In Silicon Valley, however, Nerdy Bob fits right in, designs computer systems, and commands a great deal of respect as a power-nerd. Nerdy Bob has many original scientific insights that he will prove to you in the blinking of an eye.

For example, Nerdy Bob believes that dinosaurs never died out at all, they simply got bored with mammals developing all over the place and bearing live young; to avoid these tiresome lunch companions, dinosaurs quietly evolved into birds. Brontosaurs are all around us today, he claims, flying overhead, looking down on us, and pooping on our car windshields. Nerdy Bob is also convinced that Donald Trump is the secret love child of Ronald McDonald and Leona Helmsley.

Just for fun Nerdy Bob wired all the clocks in his home to a personal computer that receives satellite transmissions from the federal atomic clocks. His clocks are now kept correct to an accuracy of a few milliseconds. Nerdy Bob's fascination with time-recording resulted in an interesting practical joke.

Nerdy Bob decided to check the accuracy of his clocks against an analemma, which is the pattern traced by daily recording the shadow cast by a fixed object at noon. Over a year the shadow will trace out a figure eight, and when it crosses the centerline each day it indicates local apparent noon. Nerdy Bob's big mistake was to try to record his experiment on the expensive hardwood floor belonging to his ingenious and fun-loving girlfriend Cathy.

Each weekend at midday Nerdy Bob would push a thumbtack into the floor to mark where the end of the window frame shadow fell. For a couple of months Cathy quietly humored him, and then she hatched a plan. After several more months of painstaking pin-placing, the shape outlined was not the expected elliptic figure eight but rather an unmistakable profile of the giant black rodent of Anaheim—Micky Mouse. The experiment was abandoned at this point.

7

Add a single sock to anyone's laundry. They'll go crazy trying to find the missing partner sock!

8

Put shaving cream instead of whipped cream on your dad's dessert trifle. What's the worst he can do—sue you? I doubt it, because *de minimis, non curat lex.**

9

Closets are an unlikely prop for funsters, but two readers wrote in to share their adventures in wardrobe-land. Stephen Shisler of Delaware described an interesting prank played in a student dormitory. Stephen's friends ordered a pizza to be delivered to dorm room #13 (there were only a dozen rooms on each floor). The jokers then ran to another part of the building and unscrewed a "1" and a "3" from two other doors.

It was the work of a minute to screw the numbers onto a broom closet door. They then filled the closet with a TV, stereo, a footlocker (serving as a desk and topped with papers and books). The stereo and TV were turned on loudly, and a student squeezed into what little space remained.

The pizza guy arrived, knocked on the door of "#13," and the occupant responded by shouting, "Just a minute!" and merely sat there. After a couple of minutes, another knock and the same reply. After repeating this a couple more times, the door opened, and the delivery-man almost fainted from surprise.

I would like to see this trick upgraded from a class 2 (surprise) to a class 3 (hoax) trick, by repeating it with a

* The law is not concerned with trifles.

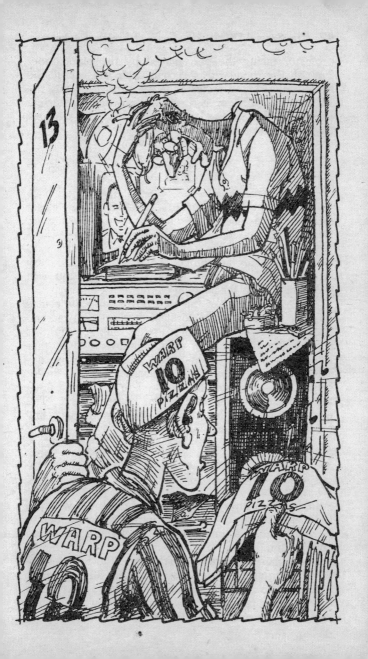

professor taking the part played by the pizza dude. Furnish the room with a second chair and extend the fun by inviting the professor in (perhaps displacing the TV into the corridor if necessary). Invent a plausible reason for the cramped accommodation, and see how far you can take this one!

10

Another practical joker to come out of the closet (practical joke-wise) is Lee Koecke, from Washington State. Lee invented the "portable closet"—a three-sided box a little larger than a door frame and about a yard deep. The sides are hinged so it folds flat for easy storage, and Lee built it so it can easily be fitted with shelves and rods for hanging clothes.

The trick works like this: whenever someone comes to visit, you set up the closet at the back of a random doorway (e.g., the entrance to the dining room). As soon as the victim is out of sight, move it to another location. Pretty soon you'll have them hopelessly confused about the layout of the house. For a grand finale, set it up just outside their room. The victim will open the door to find the rest of the house missing. The portable closet also has great possibilities for concealing rooms on a more permanent basis.

11

Jokers must always be prepared to risk the wrath of their victims, but my colleague Farley Rusks seemed to be going out on a limb when he provoked a witch into cursing him.

Farley has a contraband radar gun (the full story of how he acquired this impressive and useful implement is told in the chapter on science). He was driving north on route 128 near Salem, Massachusetts, when he was passed by a very skinny woman in a Volvo. She was doing

80 mph while looking at herself in the rearview mirror and messing with her hair.

Pride is number one of the seven deadly sins, and sinners must always be punished, so Farley zapped her with the radar gun. Bingo! He must have set off her radar detector, because she immediately hit the brakes and dropped behind. She recovered her nerve a few minutes later; as she came alongside, Farley gave her some more microwaves and let her see the pistol. Just to make it obvious Farley blew across the tip of the gun and smiled. The suspected sorceress was not amused. She started cackling and waved something at Farley that looked like a turkey wishbone wrapped in green ribbon. Farley claims that he hasn't had any bad luck yet, although a hubcap fell off his tire the next day and two weeks later he dropped a dime and it rolled down a drain. Don't tell *me* there's no karma.

12

Ever been bothered by a bandit vending machine? One that repeatedly swallows your money but refuses to hand over the goods? One friend of mine keeps a specially bent wire coat hanger for this purpose. No, not for snatching out the goods, but for placing a realistic rubber cockroach inside the machine in a prominent position.

Sales plummet, preventing further customers being ripped off, and the vending machine owners usually send an engineer to investigate right away!

13

A new variety of bogus letter has appeared to confuse and aggravate deserving recipients. You prepare a sheet that looks like the second page of a letter, the idea being to let the victim think that the sender mistakenly forgot to include the first page, which has all the juicy details. The page that the victim does get, reads as:

. . . so the IRS agents finally acted as though they were satisfied. I tell you, I've never been so thoroughly grilled before. They certainly seemed to know all about your little schemes. I'd say it's only a matter of time before they visit you too. It might look better if you turn yourself in before they get to you.

I hope you won't let this affect our friendship, whether you get things cleared up or not. I was up against the wall, what else could I do?

Good luck,
   (illegible signature)

This will really set a guilty conscience racing!

14

Some people crave fast cars, valuable antiques, or chocolate. Me, I want a player piano. I *must* have one. The player piano is a regular piano with a hidden contraption that works its own keys from inside, effectively playing with itself. Amuse your friends with your musical virtuosity for half an hour, then walk away from the keyboard, leaving it still pounding out a rattling good melody. Leave everyone foolishly singing along, entertaining a machine. You can fake a player piano with a regular piano and a tape recorder inside it.

Sing along yourself if you're a really lousy singer. It's amazing what you can get away with if the ivories are tickled fast enough. Perhaps one day the miracle of modern electronics will extend the player principle to player harmonicas, player cymbals, and for the terminally tin-eared, the player tambourine.

15

The U.S. Army recently designed new combat uniforms that replaced all of the buttons with Velcro. After everything was approved it noticed that, if you are trying to sneak up on someone, it is not such a good idea that your pocket goes RRRRIIIIIIIPP when you go to get out a grenade. The solution? Bear in mind that this was the Defense Department, so rather than return to buttons, they funded a research contract to develop stealth Velcro. Yes that's right, Velcro that doesn't go RRRRIIIPPP!

Classic Velcro is a lot more fun than stealth Velcro; stand behind a mark who is fat or wearing tight clothes, and wait until he or she bends over, then rip apart a pair of Velcro strips! A good use for this is in speeding up ski-lift lines by moving out people ahead of you.

16

Build a snowman on a street corner, in front of a fire hydrant. When the neighborhood hoodlums come by and take a flying kick at it, or even better try to knock it down with a car, well . . . you know . . . they'll be sorry.

Animal
Crackers, or
Harris Boils
the Cat

"Nature teaches beasts to know their friends"
                    Shakespeare, *Coriolanus*, Act II, sc 1.

Which came first, the chicken or the egg? Well, obviously the egg did; dinosaurs laid eggs, and there were dinosaurs around long before there were hens. Hens are a comparatively late arrival on the evolutionary scene, but eggs have gotten laid since the first multicelled invertebrates figured out how to party in pairs.

Now that we've settled that old question, let's consider the matter of animals and practical jokes. Given the choice, I'm sure most animals would much prefer to join us in a little harmless fun, rather than be devoured by us. Fortunately, to prevent too much abuse, there are animal protection groups, like the Lobster Party in eastern Canada at the last election. Their main promise was to stop the senseless slaughter of baby octopus for the little suction cups used to make shower mats and soap dish mats. Like many of the pranks here, this one is straight from the horse's ass.

17

I'm not sure if this would qualify for the David Letterman show under "stupid pet tricks" or "stupid human tricks," but my old and valued friend Nick Corder (remember Nick? Well, I'm surprised because I haven't mentioned him yet) trained his dog to run to other people when he called it.

Nick would point the victim out to the dog, then back off many feet and start summoning the dog by name. The dog would lope dutifully to the victim, circle her (Nick invariably chose a young lady as the recipient of this trick) a few times, then roll over and play dead. Nick would complete the prank by bounding up to "investigate."

Nick got more dates out of that ploy than Zsa Zsa Gabor has traffic tickets. Hmmm, maybe it wasn't such a stupid trick after all. While learning this stunt, the dog got excited once and bit Nick. We rushed him off for immediate medical attention and a rabies test. Luckily he was okay, so we came right back to see if Nick needed anything too.

18

During college Harris and I lived in a large house that we shared with several other students. One of our roommates was Charlotte, an art history major, who was also probably the most enthusiastic animal lover since Catherine the Great. Charlotte had wheedled Harris and me until we agreed to get a house pet kitten. It was arranged that Harris and I would pick one out, then Charlotte would stop by the pound later to fill out the paperwork and bring it home. Harris isn't very good with animals—he fed his tropical fish too much and they died; not from overeating but because the food displaced all the water in the aquarium.

When I met Harris at the animal shelter, I was surprised to see him wearing a chef's hat and apron. Everything became clear when he asked the shelter assistant to show him only the plumpest kittens. He would pick them each up in turn, and heft them to get an idea of weight and fatness. Though no one said anything directly, we got some pretty hard stares and brusque attention, but not nearly as much as Charlotte got when she arrived later in the day to take the kitten home.

I don't think she ever found out why the pound staff gave her so much grief. She had to sign a form promising to produce the kitten on demand in any future visit by the inspectors. She would have been mortified if

they had actually made a visit, so Harris and I set to plotting this for her too, and occasionally left bogus phone messages from the pound.

19

The cat situation didn't end there, however. It's a strange thing to come home unexpectedly and find your roommate apparently boiling the pet cat in your saucepan. Most people just don't have the life experience to help them cope with such a bizarre encounter. The situation calls for understanding, patience, tact, and diplomacy. I like to think that I displayed all of these qualities when I surprised Harris in this curious endeavor.

"Harris," I snarled. "those voices in your head, that only you can hear, are they bothering you again? What are you doing? You'll ruin my saucepan!"

"I'm dyeing the cat purple," Harris explained with great dignity. Harris has a rare gift for reducing complex situations to their simplest essentials, and I could see at once that he was right. He was dyeing the cat purple. "Latch the door, would you? I'm at a crucial stage." I did as he asked, and noticed that he had some cosmetic hair dye, which he was carefully applying with lukewarm water to the animal at one end while distracting it at the other with fresh fish. The procedure was soon complete, and we disposed of the evidence, sat back, and waited.

Charlotte hit the roof when she discovered the new colored patch on our kitten. "Perhaps it's a melanoma," I suggested helpfully. Discarding Harris's wry comment ("The things you see when you ain't got your gun!") Charlotte searched the trash until she found the hair-dye packaging. That discovery really put the "cat" in "catastrophe." It wouldn't be accurate to say that she lost control, for she never really had control in the first place. She stormed and raged, and I warned Harris that we should probably lay low for a bit until the whole thing blew over.

Harris can be as stubborn as a cucumber, so naturally he escalated to level two of the prank. Every week, he would secretly reapply a fresh coating of the dye. The kitten really began to look forward to the process, because it knew it would be rewarded with a tasty fish snack. The kitten stayed dyed for the entire semester without Charlotte being able to prove a thing. She took it home with her at Christmas, and in a few days the patch faded to its original markings. Why did Harris do it? I think it was partly because he wondered if Charlotte would notice, partly because he was interested in a scientific evaluation of the situation, but mostly because he is a rowdy yahoo who enjoys raising a ruckus.

20

Teach a parrot to say some "irregular verbs" —such as the seven dirty words that you may never print in a book,* nor say on the radio.

21

The date: April 1. The scene: a phone message has been left for you, asking you to return the call of "Mr. Baer," "Mrs. C. Lyon," etc. The action: you call the number, and (huge surprise) it turns out to be the city zoo.

This is such a common joke that most zoos actually hire extra operators on April 1 to answer the phones; not only do they answer, but they ask the person for a donation, too. People are so embarrassed at their gullibility that they often pay up.

* The seven dirty words that you may never print in a book are: peep, pipe, pimp, poop, pope, priapism, and pump.

22

Frank Reid from Indiana reports that "dog-standing" is an obscure sport practiced in Appalachia. When you spot a dead dog beside a lonely road, stop, and grab the snow shovel and clothespin that you keep in the back of your pickup truck especially for the purpose.

Put the clothespin on your nose, and slide the shovel under the dog. Move the mutt to the middle of the road, raise it to a lifelike position, and take off. If the dog stands up on the first try, it's worth ten points! If following traffic slows down to allow the deceased mutt time to run off the road, the score is doubled.

23

The renowned prankster Hugh Troy once collected an impressive number of live moths from around a porch light and took them to the local movie house in a shoe box. After the movie started he opened the box and the moths all migrated to the beam of light from the projector, thus making the film unviewable. What I've never been able to figure out is if moths like the light so much, why do they only come out at night?

The moth incident took place in a college theater, and the audience expressed its displeasure in the traditional manner of whistling, footstamping, and catcalling. The manager turned on the house lights, and the moths promptly disappeared, only to migrate back to the beam when the film restarted. Troy then saved the day with a giant butterfly net.

24

Anyone working in a laboratory generally has access to all kinds of interesting supplies and equipment. One way to give your neighbor pause for thought is to "discover" a bald (hairless) lab mouse in his basement. Then ask him if he has had his house tested for radon gas yet.

25

Robert Pilz writes in from Florida:

"When I was in the drafting department at a large research organization, a co-worker used to do some odd things in idle moments. He would take some cleaning fluid (commonly used by draftsmen) and put it into a small bottle. He would then trap a housefly in his hands, without crushing it, and put it into the bottle. The cleaning fluid had ether in it and would put the fly to sleep. Then, he would take a hair, about 5 inches long, and tie it to one of the fly's legs. Next, he would take a small strip of lightweight paper and attach it to the other end of the hair. On the paper, he would write an advertisement such as EAT AT JOE'S BAR (a local public establishment, not above question on matters of hygiene). When the fly awoke, it would fly around very slowly and the paper would stream behind, very similar to the advertising banners carried by old crop-dusters!"

Needless to add, this is only to be done by trained individuals, but do try it at home anyway.

26

The uniquely named STella from Silicon Valley has an unusual performing cat. A while ago, funds were pretty limited, and STella had a cat who liked to eat as much as anyone. How could extra funds be obtained for the kitty, so to speak? STella's solution was simple. Take a portable tape recorder over to the public library. Use it to tape a bagpipe record. Sling the tape player under one arm and the cat under the other.

Take the cat out to the busiest campus of the nearest college. Arrange the cat across your chest, head down,

and insert the end of the tail gently between your lips. Given a recorded bagpipe, it is not necessary to bite the cat's tail. Just puff out your cheeks and pretend to breathe heavily while gently massaging the cat's backbone. After you have collected a crowd, pass the hat. Then adjourn to a convenience store and buy the cat some tuna or shrimp, and yourself a sandwich and cola. Then go do it again at the next change of class.

27

STella concludes, "Cats seem to accept in good spirits being hassled by the people they own, and I've even seen cats pull practical jokes of their own—one kitten discovered that if he climbed up on the counter and stood on the button of the can opener, all the other cats would hear the sound and rush into the kitchen."

28

Place this ad in your nearest big city newspaper, with a suitable victim's phone number, then stand back and let the waves of misplaced outrage flood over him.

For sale: Attractive stuffed and mounted bottlenose dolphin. Seven feet long, professionally stuffed and mounted. I am loathe to part with this because it's a very impressive piece when it's hanging on your wall, and I had so much fun fishing for it. It put up a real fight, let me tell you, and made some weird noises when I landed it with a gaff hook. I am really fond of it. $400 or best offer."

29

Cow-tipping is a popular recreation at agricultural colleges. Aggies sneak up to sleeping cows, and gently push them over. You wouldn't catch me doing this. Watch out for bulls.

30

An old fisherman I know claimed that, as a boy, he and a bunch of other malcontents once put a live shark into the town swimming pool. The unlucky fish got tangled in the last net of the day. Sharks are typically killed when caught on fishing trips, but on this occasion they were very close to shore, and so brought it into the boat, sponging it down every fifteen minutes.

It was a simple matter to wrap the shark in a tarpaulin, drive it across town in a pickup truck, and tip it into the swimming pool. It was a small dog shark about five feet long, but it looked a whole lot bigger to anyone who saw the fin breaking the surface. It swum around menacingly for several hours until the authorities netted it once more and returned it to the ocean, none the worse for its trip.

31

During the summer of 1984 volunteers at the Atlanta Zoological Society were innundated by calls from members who had received a copy of this letter and were panicking at the prospect of what was suggested.

THE ATLANTA ZOO

Dear Mr. Green,

As you are aware, Atlanta's zoo is going through a very stressful period. The Board has considered sev-

eral alternatives and we feel we have a novel, short-
term solution to the zoo's current difficulties.

Our solution, which involves you, will immediately relieve the zoo staff of the problems of daily
caring for the animals and give the staff the opportunity to perform much needed repairs in animal
exhibits.

You have been selected to care for one of the animals for the rest of the summer. You were highly
recommended to us because of your concern for the
reputation of the Atlanta Zoo, and your known love
of animals.

Accordingly, Dixie, our North African hippopota-
mus, will soon be delivered to your home. Please
be responsible for her care, housing, and feeding until September. Our zoo veterinarian can answer any
questions regarding Dixie's special diet requirements.

You'll agree, I'm sure, that by distributing our animals among caring metro-Atlanta citizens we are
keeping our problems in "our own back yard," while
constructively working toward having one of the
finest zoological facilities in the country.

Sincerely,

Rufus Simms
Director, Animal Husbandry

The letter was personally addressed to each recipient
and neatly typed on forged but official-looking Atlanta
Zoo stationery, hand signed by the supposed sender. It
is, of course, a complete hoax. They never did track
down "Rufus Simms." Could too much caffeine be the
real villain here? Notice that this prank and Coca-Cola's
headquarters are both in Atlanta. Mere coincidence? I
think not.

Sassing
Ann Landers

Mellow nuts have the hardest rind
Sir Walter Scott, *Lord of the Isles, canto 3*

If you read the newspaper the way I do, then the bottom of your pet's litter tray probably sees more of the daily tabloid than either of us. There's one type of newspaper story that always gets my attention, however: anything to do with practical jokes. That's why I was so excited to see a series of these turn up in Ann Landers' newspaper column. But I'm getting a little ahead of myself here.

Esther and Pauline Friedman are identical twins from the Midwest who, under the pen names Ann Landers and Abby Van Buren, have had a thirty-five-year lock on newspaper advice columns. Esther (Ann Landers) and Pauline (Dear Abby) are, literally, the sob sisters of America. In 1955, Esther got the job of continuing the well-established "Ann Landers" column in the *Chicago Sun-Times*. At first the twins wrote the column together, but their cooperation sadly seemed to turn to bitterness when, after a few months, Pauline started up the competing "Dear Abby" column in the *San Francisco Chronicle*. The newfound rivalry between the sisters ignited a private feud that sometimes spilled over into public and has continued to this day. As Pauline's husband once exclaimed, "If these are twin sisters, I'll take cobras!"

The two columns, "Ann Landers" and "Dear Abby," quickly grew in popularity and were carried by more and more newspapers. For more than thirty years now the two have been syndicated across America, vicariously solving the problems of their correspondents.

32

A spate of letters about practical jokes appeared in Ann Landers' columns and, to my surprise, Ann was dead set against them. Ann seems to take a peculiar, almost perverse, delight in letting a correspondent describe a practical joke so that she can then denounce it, as in the following letters:

> Dear Ann,
>   You said that obscene bumper stickers are not against the law. In Florida they are! An obscene bumper sticker is a second-degree misdemeanor punishable by six months in jail!

Well, yes, and in other parts of the uncivilized world they also cut your hands off for coveting your neighbor's wife's ass, but that's no reason to recommend it here. The series continues with:

> Dear Ann,
>   We were at a cocktail party, and the hostess asked, "How did you and your husband meet?" Before I could say anything, my husband said, with a perfectly straight face, "Doris was a hooker."

Ann sternly denounced such levity:

> Tell that clown he better set the record straight!

Set the record straight? Like, someone was taken in by this snappy ad lib to a nosy question? In December 1988, Ann railed against the neighbor who sneaked into a correspondent's bedroom and planted a pair of lace panties between the sheets as a joke:

> In my opinion something is fundamentally wrong with people who enjoy embarrassing or humiliating others. Call me a sourpuss, but I think practical jokes are for the birds.

Well, in *my* opinion something is fundamentally wrong with people who *don't* enjoy seeing a little good-natured embarrassment or humiliation.

33

Ann's approach to humor brings one great benefit: she finds it very hard to distinguish the bogus letters. In September 1989, a reader from Nebraska wrote to say that she had named her twin heifers "Ann" and "Abby."

Ann swallowed this bait whole, and sent her congratulations in print to her namesake in Nebraska. Though the letter writer outlined the cows' fate with some relish, the non-bovine Ann had obviously failed to note that the heifers ended up as quarter-pound hamburgers; surely one of the few occasions when Ann has been grilled in such a tasteful way.

34

One intriguing story about Ann Landers that crops up repeatedly concerns the Yale connection. Ann has often reported how she was subjected to a spate of bogus letters from undergraduates at Yale University, how she spotted the hoax at once, and sent back good-natured replies. Everyone knows that Ann dealt with the Yale incident magnificently, and came out of it smelling of roses.

But maybe everyone is wrong. The more I investigated this incident, the less I could find to support Ann's story. I contacted the Yale dean of student affairs, the main libraries, the Yale Office of Public Information, the Yale President's Office, the university historian, the alumni magazine, the biographers of Ann, and Ann Landers herself. Ann never replied to my note and, curiously, most of the others had heard of the alleged episode, but none of them could supply any hard facts.

More research led to a surprising theory. The *Yale Daily News* quizzed Ann on this very topic in 1983, and her comments were revealing: "Heaven knows how many letters I've received from Yale. Over these twenty-seven years I would say hundreds . . ."

In other words, maybe there never was any one Yale incident! Did Ann Landers build the story up out of her ongoing mailbag? An uncharitable observer might conclude that she wildly exaggerated the Yale connection to gain media attention ("Celebrity beats the wits of our finest university!"). This would be no different from a politician manipulating a crisis for favorable news coverage, or even a practical joke book author coming up with wild theories about media personalities to get some free publicity. Er, no, on second thought, it's nothing like that.

35

Every few years Ann and her sister Abby break their vow of silence toward each other long enough to deny that they feud. Nobody believes them. But what sort of a way to behave is this? I wrote to Ann asking her advice on such a family problem, but describing her own circumstances of the sisterly feud, as though they were mine:

Dear Ann,
    My own sister runs a counselling service that competes with my own business. To top it off, she says mean things about me behind my back! I have stopped speaking to her.
    Should I swallow my pride and make up with her? I feel such an old phoney; people come to me for wisdom and I can't even work out my own family problems. What's your advice?

No answer! Despite Ann's oft-repeated claim that every letter is answered, on this occasion answer came there none!

36

This ploy was too good to let rest, so I tried the very same question on her sister. For the Dear Abby version, I was able to add the additional (true) information:

My sister even had cosmetic surgery on her nose and butt, but she still pokes her nose into other people's business and is a major-league buttinsky.

Unlike her sister, Abby obviously got it, because she sent a quick reply saying "Hey, if you tried to make it up with her then it's *her* problem!" My question never suggested any such thing! This is the sort of thing you frequently see at the movies, which is why psychiatrists call it "projection."

37

So far the score was tied between anxiety queens and practical jokers. I decided to up the ante somewhat, and discussed the situation with expert pranksters Harris Tweed and "Nerdy" Bob Byteswap. They both appreciated the challenge and set to work. Nerdy Bob's endeavor soon sucked in Ann Landers. He merely sent her a question that is so stupid that no one could possibly take it seriously. On November 4, 1989, Ann duly published Nerdy Bob's polite inquiry:

Can you please tell me what time it is? There are clocks everywhere, but unfortunately no two have the same time.

Ann answered it seriously, by refering to an eminent authority on time:

> The National Institute of Standards and Technology tells us "Coordinated Universal Time" is the scientific standard. You can call the institute at (303) 499-7111. The exact time is announced once every minute.

Nerdy Bob was not impressed. He sniffily remarked that phone propagation delays could cause these (and any dialup time services) to be off by *as much as 30 milliseconds*.

38

While Nerdy Bob's attempt was good, and it fooled Ann, Harris came up with a real class 1 practical joke. Harris deserves the golden toilet chain with crossed legs for this one. His brilliantly innocent suggestion and Ann's artless response appeared in her nationally syndicated column on July 14, 1989.

> Dear Ann, I have a terrific suggestion for removing grease and grime from the hands and face. Take a cup of lard and add 5 tablespoons of sugar: Mix well and use like soap. You'll be amazed at the results!

I warned Harris that his final sentence was a dead giveaway, but apparently I was wrong, for Ann printed the "hint" in full and replied:

> I did try it and it works quite well. Thanks for sharing.

Well, cleanliness *is* next to godliness. I'll just bet it does wonders for the complexion too! The thought of Ann smearing animal fat on her face at Harris's sugges-

tion, and then passing on the idea to an astonished nation, was almost too much for us. We still occasionally get fits of hysteria when we pass the fats section in the supermarket.

The
Misappliance
of Science

"Our investigations have always contributed more to our amusement than they have to our knowledge."

Will Rogers, *Autobiography*.

Good practical joking, like good science, requires imagination and persistence. Do you think for a minute that the great scientists dropped their pet theories in the face of contradictory evidence and tried something else?

Well, actually, of course they did, since the essence of scientific inquiry is to construct theories that explain the observed facts. If there are observations that are not explained by a theory, then the theory must be revised or replaced. Or you can hire a graduate student to dummy up some new readings. A scientist then makes predictions based on the new theory, and devises experiments to produce new observations, which in turn will support or refute the theory. This process continues until the grant money runs out.

But science doesn't know everything. Science doesn't know why creatures with eight legs (spiders, lobsters, octopuses) are disgusting to eat. Science doesn't explain why you can't smell snot even though you have wads of it up your nose. Science can't say for sure why people eat Parmesan cheese, even though it smells like vomit, nor why it is that polite people never mention this.

Practical joking is similar to science in that both involve drawing conclusions to explain the observed evidence. The joker supplies suitable "evidence" and the victim ends up with the same kind of grip on reality that Shirley MacLaine enjoys. As Professor Einstein remarked "one must be open-minded—but not so open-minded that one's brains fall out."

39

Farley Rusks, who zapped the witch in the "New Classic Fun" chapter, proudly boasts that setting off other peoples' radar detectors is absolutely the best trick he's ever invented! Farley used his engineering expertise to build his own radar gun. A modern (superheterodyne) radar detector contains a "local oscillator" that generates a few milliwatts of microwaves. Farley's radar phaser pistol works by enhancing that effect. He bought a used radar detector in pieces and retuned the local oscillator to the police radar-gun frequency.

Farley is a genuinely creative individual, so he didn't stop there. He bought a toy plastic space pistol for 50 cents at a garage sale, and installed the whole thing inside it! He then added a 9-volt battery and a piezoelectric noisemaker from Radio Shack. The device will trigger other peoples' "fuzzbusters" up to a quarter mile away, even if they are pointed in the opposite direction. It will not interfere with real police radar, since it is merely an enhanced radar detector. It is no different in principle to the burglar alarms or automatic door openers that also set off radar detectors. (Hint!) Nonetheless, the authorities would surely not smile upon this freelance engineering hack.

Farley named it "Ronald" because all ray guns are named Ronald, just as all pythons are named Monty. Farley says he likes to think of it as a vector-subtraction device—if the speedster with the radar detector is ahead, it sucks him backward; if he's behind, it pushes him away. Besides providing an interesting diversion on long trips, it has genuinely practical applications in opening up gaps in traffic and harmlessly persuading reckless drivers to moderate their speed.

40

If you take a Rubik's Cube and turn the top level one-eighth of a turn, you can pry up and remove one of the middle edge-pieces on that level. After prying one piece off, you can put it back inverted and make the puzzle impossible to solve. People who know how to solve it are driven crazy by this.

I once acquired a "Rubik's cube" that is actually a solid piece of plastic, colored and with notches cut to make it look like the real thing. It cannot be twisted. It's fun handing it to an unsuspecting person. ("This seems a little stiff, Ruprecht. Perhaps you can use your superior strength to force it.") Somehow it always remains "solved."

41

There are really only three colleges to consider if you are serious about practical jokes: Caltech and MIT if you're good enough to study science; Yale if you're rich enough not to have to. A few years ago a group of California Institute of Technology underclassmen decided to take revenge on one particular senior. They "borrowed" a crane and lifted his BMW up onto the roof of a building. But the crowning touch, and the picture that made the newspapers, was the security guard up on the roof writing out a parking ticket! Reason: "not parked in a marked space."

42

In one MIT dormitory, "octagon" parties became quite a tradition. The name came from a huge eight-sided concrete planter that was manhandled up and down the hall each hour during the party. The vibrations, as the heavy structure thudded along, reverberated through the entire building. The design of the dormitory was such that vibrations were hardly noticeable on the third floor, but the fifth floor rocked like an Elvis concert.

The parties came to an abrupt end when the authorities discovered the illicit use of the planter, and it was removed to a more distant and harmless location.

43

The previous story is a good one, but my favorite anecdote about resonance involves the scientist Nikola Tesla and the writer Mark Twain. Twain was an active prankster himself, responsible for more than one fake newspaper report. On this occasion, however, he was the butt of the joke.

Tesla was experimenting in his New York laboratory with a platform that vibrated at the resonant frequency of the human body. It was pleasurable to stand on for a couple of minutes; it then brought on an urgent need to run for the bathroom. Tesla invited Twain to try this latest development. He didn't tell Twain what it was except to say it would cause a big revolution in every hospital and home.

Twain stood happily on the platform, enjoying the novelty, when suddenly the laxative effect kicked in, his whole expression changed, and he sprinted for the bathroom. Tesla never developed this interesting device beyond a prototype, so the predicted revolutionary "movement" never materialized.

44

Astounding class 1 practical joke effects can be obtained with frozen shaving cream. Freeze a can by immersing it in liquid nitrogen. Your home freezer doesn't get nearly cold enough, but liquid nitrogen is common in many physics laboratories. Or you can try

"Cryogenics" in the Yellow Pages. Once the shaving cream is frozen solid the can is peeled off (wear a face mask and gloves), leaving a cylinder of solid compressed foam. If you try to peel the can off before the foam is frozen, there'll be a "whoosh" noise and suddenly you'll be looking like Frosty the Snowman.

When the foam thaws, it expands to dozens of times the volume. Five cans of frozen shaving cream are enough to fill and lightly pressurize a compact car. I learned of this trick from a friend-of-a-friend who actually did it. I still visit him from time to time in Folsom prison.

45

Have you ever seen a "panic box"? This is a small box with a big red button and a label reading:

PANIC BUTTON
DO NOT PRESS!

The one I saw also had a power cord plugged into the nearest outlet, and a prominent on/off switch. It looked a little like a fire alarm, except that it was obviously self-contained, and quite small.

It generally doesn't take long for a curious passerby to press the button. Immediately a built-in Klaxon starts a hair-raising scream. Naturally the poor sucker would flip the switch off—only to find that the switch was a dummy! Then the sucker would yank out the power cord—that was a dummy too! By this time a small crowd had normally gathered, and the nosy person would begin to look quite uncomfortable.

The thing was internally powered with a 9-volt battery and used a magnetic reed switch to turn it off. Eventually the owner would pick it up and turn it off with a magnet from his pocket. The crowd would slowly disperse, but the original unfortunate was usually long gone. It was great!

46

Sir Arthur Conan Doyle based his character Sherlock Holmes on a Scottish pathology professor, Dr. Joseph Bell. One of Dr. Bell's favorite tricks was to lecture to a class with a glass of urine next to him. Cautioning the class to observe him closely, he would dip a finger into the sample and apparently taste it. The professor would then invite selected medical students to repeat the experiment.

After the class had had about all the entertainment they could stand, the good professor would warn them again on the necessity for observation and reveal that he dipped his middle finger into the glass, but tasted his index finger. Professors aren't what they used to be, for which we are all very grateful.

47

The French mathematician Pierre de Fermat is most famous for what has come to be known as "Fermat's Last Theorem." After his death, a notebook of his was found, giving a mathematical conjecture that remains unproven to this day, namely that

$$x^n + y^n = z^n$$

has solutions for integer values of x, y, z, n only when n is less than 3. Fermat had written at the side of the page: "I have discovered a truly wonderful proof of this, which this margin is unfortunately too small to contain!" Was Fermat in earnest, or was he was pulling the august legs of the entire mathematical community?

From the perspective of an experienced trickster, I am convinced that Fermat was pulling a fast one here. First, he was an outsider among the mathematical community, even labelled as a "troublemaker" by Descartes. This establishes a motive for revenge.

Second, if you're penning a reminder to yourself, you

might write "I have discovered a truly wonderful proof of this," but what possible reason would you have for adding "which this margin is too small to contain"? You know that well enough; the only possible reason for mentioning the inadequate margin is to convince other people that you know something, even though you didn't write it down. This establishes that Fermat intended his note to be found and read by others.

Finally, three-and-a-half centuries of intense research by better mathematicians have failed to duplicate the proof that Fermat claimed he found. This points to a scam. Pierre de Fermat, medieval mischief maker, what a guy!

Funnily enough, this reminds me that I have discovered a wonderful new proof of the Unified Field theory. This theory is a holy grail long sought by physicists, and it reconciles the four fundamental forces of nature (the strong nuclear force, the weak nuclear force, gravity, and levity). Unfortunately the proof is too long to include in this chapter. Perhaps it will be in the Third Official Handbook of Practical Jokes (don't count on it).

48

Things were quiet at work. Too quiet. I had done nothing interesting to Nerdy Bob for almost a month. I'd listened patiently to his latest theory that he called "the equation of dreams," which states:

$$\text{what you eat} - \text{what you think} = \text{what you dream}$$

It made sense in a crazy kind of way; dreams are indigestible parts of food being resolved by the subconscious. In return for listening to this farrago I decided to fix Nerdy Bob's office clock so that it would run backward. There are two simple ways to fix an electric clock to run counterclockwise. The synchronous motors in most clocks will happily run in either direction (based on where in the sine wave the power is when you plug it in). There is a spring that prevents the spindle from rotating counterclockwise. Detach the spring, and spin the motor in the desired direction with your finger and thumb.

The other method is even simpler, if you're used to lateral thinking. All analog clocks run counterclockwise if you look from behind. So simply unbolt the movement and bolt it on the other way round. As with all electrical equipment, there are three precautions you must always follow: (1) disconnect the power before making any modifications; (2) restrict yourself to battery-driven clocks until you know what you're doing; and (3) wait till your mom goes out shopping before starting this little project.

When Nerdy Bob noticed my improvement, his first act was to listen intently to the clock to see whether it was now making a "kcot kcit" sound.

49

Take an ordinary balloon, put a little crushed dry ice in it, and tie the end. Stuff the balloon in the back pocket of somebody's pants before they put them on (perhaps your brother while he is still asleep).

As the dry ice sublimates (heats up and converts to vapor), the victim's butt will transform into interesting shapes without him noticing. He will find out about this when he tries to sit down, but the balloon will then be too large to remove without drastic measures.

50

In the late 1970s pocket calculators were still huge and clunky, though inexpensive. Farley Rusks got hold of an old one that featured a small red light used to indicate errors. He rewired the lines going to the light to a micro-relay, and wired the relay to a battery, flashbulb, and a coil of wire in a small can of chemical

that, when heated by the coil, would emit clouds of white smoke. This chemical was obtained at a hobby shop, where it was sold to provide realistic looking smoke for model trains.

The calculator was quite large enough to accommodate these extra parts, and when you did something in error (like divided by zero), you would get the same result that the folks on the *Enterprise* got when their computers malfunctioned! This went over very well with the other students, who were for the most part StarTrek fans. The design was then modified to get sparks and noise, but unfortunately Farley burned down the east wing of the school in the attempt! Just kidding! It was actually the west wing.

51

Fill any inflatable, not with air but with helium. We used an inflatable pterodactyl and left it zooming around someone's office, no strings attached.

Look up "balloons" in the Yellow Pages, then call the shops to find out if you can bring your own balloon in for them to fill. Helium is the inert, and therefore safe, lighter-than-air gas used today to provide buoyancy. Don't use hydrogen (this was the mistake the *Hindenberg* made).

52

Apply photocopier toner (black powder) to anything with a matt black surface, such as a telephone earpiece. It is best applied in small quantities with a paintbrush or an aspirator. On binocular eyepieces it gives the dupe raccoon eyes. Toner powder is an inert substance composed of about equal parts of styrene acrylate copolymer and iron oxide, with about 1 percent salicylic acid chromium to help it flow. Despite urban legends to the contrary, there is no specific handling hazard except in the case of klutzes.

This prank can be followed up with a zinger, just by planting trick black soap in the washroom. Then remove the elbow joint from the sink. You'll split a kidney laughing at all these zingers. When the victim finally gets the washroom straightened out, let's hope he knows to wash off with cold water. Hot water will cause toner to fuse to the surface being washed!

53

My brother Paul works as a geologist on an oil rig. He tells me that he was logging samples from the ocean floor one day, when he noticed his project leader mix a spoonful of coffee powder in with the drillings. Paul was surprised at this unorthodox procedure, but said nothing.

The sample was passed it to the chief logging geologist for further comment. Hunched over it, the chief excitedly noted "small crystalline fragments of a brown aggregate, easily crushed, appears water soluble . . ." The prankster cunningly remarked that it appeared to be a "Maxwellian layer, or possibly Nescafeian," but the poor chief still didn't cotton on, and excitedly cabled the head office with news of this unusual rock layer. They both got kicked off the rig for this one, while my brother was promoted. Moral: Never blow the whistle when you see a stunt in progress.

54

A common high-school science trick is locker rigging. Take an old stereo tape deck and the longest continuous-loop cartridge you can find. Wire up a battery, solenoid, and tone decoder to one of the playback channels of the cassette deck. On that channel, record a tone that triggers the solenoid, and on the other channel, record your voice, so that when you play it back, you can intersperse solenoid activation and voice messages. Mount the whole thing in your locker so that the solenoid plunger bangs on the locker door. Start the tape.

See how many people you can get to pay attention to a locker where somebody keeps pounding on the door and yelling, "Help! Let me out." It's even more fun when they finally cut the lock off and open the door to find a note saying something pleasant on it. If you are able to sneak it into the staff room, with a timer to turn it on after 30 minutes, this provides entertainment unrivaled outside Wednesday night Jell-O wrestling.

Zinger or boomerang (it's up to you): the school principal usually sends any telltale remains to the physics department for analysis. Make sure that you are well prepared in advance: either leave no telltale identification, or preferably leave bogus evidence that fingers someone else (an addressed envelope, ID card, or the like), or just plan to steal the evidence back.

55

The Reuben H. Fleet Science Museum is a terrific museum to visit if you're ever in San Diego. Most of their exhibits require you to operate something, and they all have little explanatory notices describing exactly what you are supposed to do and to notice. Someone on the staff has extended this exhibit policy to the drinking fountain, which is labeled:

WATER FOUNTAIN—A device for drinking
Find the little round button and push it down. Water should pour from the assembly on top. The water comes out so it is just out of reach of your mouth, and at an angle so you must make funny faces to get your lips wet.

Notice also how the guard and nozzle are shaped to prevent anyone getting close enough to drink. The height is carefully measured to be too tall for kids and too short for adults.

The curator saw me laughing at this, and said that they originally put the sign up because many visitors did not bother to read any instructions. Instructions on unlikely objects tended to draw attention. He also said that they were installing a new exhibit like a phone booth, and the object was to get inside. It was deliberately set up to be impossible to enter, unless you read the instructions right to the end before starting.

A good idea, but I don't think they carried it quite far enough—I would arrange the exhibit so that it penalized those who did not read the instructions, by squirting cold water onto them while simultaneously playing a loud tape that drew attention to the victim's plight ("Bong! Ha! Ha! Ha! Another loser who can't READ!").

56

Frank rigged a drinking fountain in another way. A fountain at work bothered him by being too close to his office. He simply put up an official-looking sign next to it, reading, UNIVERSAL UNISEX URINALS, DRINK AT YOUR OWN RISK. Patronage dropped off to zero within a few hours.

57

In the first Handbook, I pointed out what a scam Super Glue is, in that it doesn't seem to glue anything except your fingers. Luckily, my pal Charlie had an explanation, a suggestion, and a bonus new practical joke. The explanation is that Super Glue was originally *designed* to glue human skin! It was intended as a replacement for sutures, although it never was very good at this either.

The suggestion is that there are several ways to improve the adhesion of Super Glue. You can slightly moisten the surfaces to be joined (breathing on them is enough, the water vapor in your breath will do the trick); you can lay a line of baking soda in a crack you want filled and glued (this seems to work because baking soda is made up of sharp angular crystals that give the glue something to grip); or you can use the "zip kicker" spray from a hobby store that sets Super Glue instantly.

Charlie's bonus practical joke involved asking someone for their hand in marriage, and at the same time using Super Glue on your palm to ensure that the two of you would be united for the immediate future, even if the answer was no. I think this idea goes a long way toward explaining why Charlie is still a bachelor at this time.

58

In a letter to *Physics Today*, scientist Allen D. Allen described a novel computer application that saved a lot of his time. He explained that he received several letters a week containing "refutations" of the Special Theory of Relativity. Allen discovered that the errors in these letters usually fell into one of a small number of classes.

He wrote a computer program to deal with this. Now he scans through the correspondence, types in the identifying number of the fallacy, and the computer automatically generates a reply custom-tailored to the victim—er, correspondent. The program has a data base of ten reply paragraphs that correct the ten most common fallacies in understanding Einstein's Special Theory of Relativity.

Are you following all this, or should I write slower? Usually Allen's letter of correction will only contain a couple of these paragraphs. Some people say that there are only three laws of physics namely, force = mass * acceleration, things fall down, and you can't push a rope. I think Allen's data base shows that it's a bit more complicated:

1. Your theory is equivalent to the theory that
   [previous theory (e.g., ether drag) printed here]
   which was proposed by

[original proponents printed here]

This theory was rejected then (as it must be now) because

[experimental evidence contradicting theory printed here]

2. A frame is preferred if and only if the laws of physics inside that frame are different from the laws applying outside the frame. But a frame is *not* preferred just because it is a cosmic frame or a big frame or a pretty frame. To argue that a frame is preferred you must show how the laws of physics are different inside the frame than they are outside the frame.

3. You have not adequately explained the most important (to physicists) transformation of all, which is the transformation of mass. This Lorentz transformation is very real—as real as nuclear power—and not just a matter of arbitrary coordinates. As you may know, mass transformation and time transformation are related under conservation of momentum $P = FT = MAT$. Thus both transformations are very real and are not merely a way of talking about things.

4. Time dilation is observed in experiments that do not involve light propagation or coordinate transformation if laboratory clocks tick off time T as a muon ensemble flies from source to detector. The muon aging is determined by a direct measurement at the detector, and not by transporting information across a distance. Hence, time dilation is not just an abstraction or an artifact resulting from Einstein's operational definitions.

5. Einstein's theory of relativity was a correction to Newton's theory, which is also relativistic. The views of the addressee contradict the theories of both Newton and Einstein. For example, $X - VT$ means that if you are driving down the road at 90 km/hr, the windshield of your car maintains its distance from your head, even though the telephone poles

along the road do not. This is not a matter of arbitrary interpretation but involves a certain physical reality that can mean the difference between life and death.

6. You have been thrown off by Einstein's remarks on signaling. These remarks were intended to provide a philosophical viability to the lack of absolute simultaneity in the special theory of relativity, and are not really central to the theory itself. In this regard, the theory simply assumes the usual expression for speed and assumes the speed of light is frame-independent. This is *equivalent* to Lorentz time dilation and the rest follows very simply with no need for any kind of mumbo jumbo.

7. The special theory of relativity does *not* say that the speed of light is independent of its source. The wave nature of light says that. The theory says that the speed of light is *frame-independent*. This might be wrong because the speed of light might be transformed in a strongly nonlinear fashion. However, we know that the speed of light is not $C' = V + C$ from two experiments: (a) Michelson-Morley and (b) starlight aberration (which tells us that the earth does not drag some ether along with it). Thus theories proposing $C' = V + C$ are contradicted by (a) and (b). Ballistic theories of light actually have ittle to do with the Special Theory of Relativity and are contradicted by the first principles of ordinary physics.

8. You are familiar with the formal form of the special theory of relativity developed by Minkowski but not the underlying physics due to Einstein, as indicated in part by the other paragraphs of this analysis.

9. Your conceptualizations are too confused for analysis.

10. Look up the meaning of the word "absolute." It means independent of a reference system (or frame) as in absolute value, absolute units, absolute temperature, and such. A parameter is therefore not "absolute" unless everyone agrees on its magnitude (e.g., light speed is absolute in the special theory of

relativity). If by "motion" you mean P/M, then it is obvious that motion is frame-dependent and so there can not be an absolute frame for motion. However, there might be a *preferred* frame (at least in principle).

What used to take Allen hours now takes only moments. Furthermore, the automated response is always purely technical, unbiased, and consistent.

It's bad enough to receive junk mail in the first place, but there's something hilarious about someone getting computer-generated junk mail that corrects his or her mistakes.

Love is such a funny thing
It's very like a lizard
It twines itself around the heart
And penetrates your gizzard

Anon.

Plato described love as "the great mental disorder," but modern thinking holds that he was full of it in this pronouncement. In any case, he wasn't very experienced—all his relationships were Platonic.

When they say "all's fair in love and war," they actually mean everything is unfair, but it's no use complaining about it. The main aim is to bring pleasure to others' lives, and your own, and not to break any hearts in the process. When people are asked what they like in the opposite sex, "a sense of humor" is always one of the first things on the list. So if you can't win a partner with your charming smile or family inheritance, perhaps you can do it with one of these laughables.

59

There is an old wedding tradition of having the groom throw the bride's garter to the ushers. The groom first kneels in front of the seated bride and carefully removes her garter, then tosses it over his shoulder for one of the ushers to catch.

I saw this ceremony performed at the wedding of a *very* close friend of mine, let's call him "Joe" (not my real name). Well in advance "Joe" had concealed a lurid pair of polka-dotted boxer shorts up his sleeve. Then when "Joe" removed the bride's garter, I—er, Joe—palmed it and in a smooth movement pulled the boxers out and waved them around in the air.

Total pandemonium immediately broke out. No amount of sugar could have caused a rush like this! The bride was frantically checking whether the groom really had taken her panties, the best man was trying to restrain the mother of the bride from throttling the groom, and a dish ran away with the spoon.

60

My buddy Bil* has been crossed in love more often than the ballroom floor of the Ritz Hotel, although he gets waxed less often. He is no stud-muffin, but at least he tries. As a fourth-year student in college, he fell madly for a freshman coed. Maureen was an art student, and in a sudden fit of creativity, Bil stuck a dried apricot into an envelope. With all the misplaced confidence of the Jamaican bobsled team, Bil signed it "Love, Vincent" and, in a move that can only be described as Freudian, stuffed it into her mail slot.

No one had ever mentioned to Bil that the recipient of van Gogh's ear was a whore, an historical fact that Maureen apparently was aware of but not amused by. Bil and Maureen did not elope and get married that spring, nor did they live happily ever after.

Bil later tried to patch it up by sending the object of his desires some flowers. Since the days of Helen of Troy, women have tended to "beware of Geeks bearing gifts." I think he might have had more luck if he hadn't chosen, in another fit of clashing symbolism, Venus flytraps.

* Why do many of my friends spell their names in strange and unusual ways? I don't know.

61

When we last met Harris in the first Handbook, he had just got married, coped with the "disappearing bridal bed," and was happily playing tunes on the Hong Kong phone system. Harris went on a whirlwind round-the-world honeymoon, and stopped off in Britain to buy a suit of armor—an item that he had always coveted but never before had the opportunity to purchase. Harris was then faced with the unexpected but expensive problem of shipping this heavy, valuable, and delicate object back home to Hong Kong.

Lateral thinking saved the day. Harris decided to put the suit of armor on, and *wear* it home. He quickly discovered that people were a lot smaller in the Middle Ages, and that he didn't have a hope of getting into the suit. It would however fit his diminutive wife. An evil glint came into Harris's eye. Harris decided to play it from the romantic angle, and in his most flagrant abuse of intelligence since the previous week told his new bride, "I'm your knight in shining armor, right? Well this is your new going-away outfit."

Once she got over the novelty of the idea, Harris's wife took to it like a real trooper—she swore at him. But Harris was adamant, and eventually she agreed. When the time came to leave she donned the chain-mail and armor, and threw a raincoat and pants over the top. Everything went smoothly until they reached the security check at the airport. The metal detector went into overdrive. The guards were astounded, and made her take it all off. At length they were satisfied, and let the couple pass. At this point Harris's wife realized she had an eighteen-hour flight ahead of her, and her chances of curling up and getting some rest were about the same as Sonny's chances of a reconciliation with Cher. "Relax," ordered Harris. "I'll help you make it through the knight!"

They reached Hong Kong in the end, and Harris's wife suffered no lasting ill effects except for a lingering interest in bondage that persists to this day. As they

went through Customs, they were asked if they had anything to declare. Harris replied in the negative and they were waved on, until his wife made a clanking noise in walking off. Again they went through the strip-search routine, mostly because Harris insisted on explaining that his wife was a dedicated heavy metal fan. In fact, she was Iron Maiden's number-one supporter.

The Customs people let them go in the end, and Harris has the suit of armor prominently displayed in his hallway to this day. He has to dust it himself, however, because his wife won't go near it. The only mail she'll touch in future, she vows, is that from the Post Office.

62

Bill Gates is chairman of the Microsoft Corporation, and one of America's youngest corporate billionaires. He has taken his company to the highest pinnacles of success through a combination of boldness, imagination, and a thorough technical background. Gates exhibited these qualities at an early age, before he had even graduated from high school. He earned some spare cash by doing some computer programming for the school administration. Gates was given the job of programming the school class schedule that assigned students to particular classes. He did a good job on this, and the program was put into immediate use.

Unknown to the school authorities, Gates had added an important modification on his own initiative. When the program scheduled a student, it checked to see if the name was "Gates." If it was, then that student was left till last. At that point, for each course where Gates had a choice of classes, the program assigned him to the one with the largest number of female students.

This is an ingenious ploy, but it boomeranged on the Gates family several years later, when Bill's younger sister started in the same school. When asked how she liked the school she replied that it was fine, but she found it hard to meet boys, because all her classes seemed to be full of female students.

63

The late actor and author David Niven told the story of the time a telephone wrong number almost led to a date for him. He called a lady he knew in Manhattan, but got a wrong number, and received a young society mademoiselle. Niven, an unknown at that time, liked the sound of the lady's voice, and tried to talk her into having lunch with him. He allayed her doubts by suggesting that she meet him at the corner of Madison and 61st. Niven would make himself recognizable by wearing a blue scarf and a red carnation. The mademoiselle could then inspect him before deciding to make contact.

Niven accordingly waited at the designated corner for two hours. During this time fifteen separate women walked by and called out his name, each of whom was no more than a plant from the real dater. Niven realized he had met his match however when he found himself being serenaded by an entire singing telegram group from Western Union.

Happy lunchtime to you (reprise three times)
Happy lunchtime Mr. Niven, etc. etc.

Very funny. Don't let it happen to you.

64

Terry is like a proud example of that virile symbol of national pride, the big-balled eagle. When Terry came to spend some vacation with me in California, I knew it was my federal duty to show him a good time. Accordingly, I called my attractive model friend Candy and asked her to substitute for my regular housecleaning service at a prearranged time.

Terry and I were at home enjoying a leisurely beer, when the doorbell rang and there was Candy, ready to do the housework. Except she was dressed in a French maid's uniform that left *rien à l'imagination*. I guess Joanne of Arc was the original French maid, but let me tell you Candy was equally aflame with passion. I told Terry that all cleaning services in California were like this, and that you could choose the type of uniform for the domestic to wear. It cost a little extra, but it's always worth paying for quality.

Candy had brought a little hand-held vacuum cleaner, and when she referred to it as her "bust-duster," I thought Terry was going to faint dead away. The blood rushed completely from his head and down into his brain.

I set Candy to work ironing a few shirts. "You don't mind if Candy does the ironing here in the living room with us, do you, Terry?" I inquired anxiously. Terry didn't mind in the least. In fact like the gentleman that he is, he insisted on helping her. Talk about "king leer"—Terry's eyes bugged out like a trout gaping for a fly. But that was, after all, the idea. He does lousy ironing, by the way.

65

Terry recovered from this setup at warp speed, and soon got his revenge. We were taking an airline flight, and under the guise of stretching his legs, Terry passed the flight attendant a note that he told her was from me. The note read "Hi! I'm independently wealthy! Where should I pick you up for dinner tonight?"

Flight attendants get hundreds of propositions in the line of duty, and they have many ways of letting the propositioner know that the attention is unwelcome. When I asked her if all the little bumps in flight made her airsick, she said it wasn't the little bumps, it was all the big jerks. I couldn't understand why I was getting such a cold shoulder, until Terry confessed hours later. Liven up any boring flight by passing the attendants unusual notes supposedly from the passengers around you.

66

One wedding was made especially memorable by the best man's speech. He started out by commenting on how wild the groom had been as a bachelor, and how all the girls would miss him now that he's unavailable. It was even said that, on occasion, the groom had been known to pass out the key to his apartment.

The best man then said that the groom was now trying to retrieve all the keys, and asked if anyone present had one. At that cue almost all the women present came forward and dropped a key on the table in front of the best man. It brought a lot of laughs, except from the bride.

67

Sometimes friends of the groom feel a responsibility to trash the bridal bedchamber. Although I don't condone this rather mean-spirited behavior, I can tell you how to gain access. First, phone all the hotels in the area, claiming to be a florist wanting to deliver flowers to the happy couple. When you find the hotel that acknowledges their reservation, a personal visit is in order.

The best man and bridesmaid can go along and register as the bridal couple! The woman should pay for the room with a charge card. Naturally the name won't match the groom's name, and the hotel reception staff will assume it is the wife's maiden name. This gives you access to the room; use it to place flowers and a champagne bottle therein.

68

William Horace De Vere Cole was an Englishman who dedicated his entire life to practical jokes, both simple and elaborate. When one of his closest friends decided to marry, everyone feared that Cole would disrupt the ceremony with some memorable surprise. The families were on tenterhooks throughout the service, but everything proceeded with the utmost decorum.

The new bride and her groom stepped outside the church, when suddenly it happened. A gorgeous young woman, clutching a young baby, flung herself in front of the groom, and tragically, dementedly swore her undying love to the new groom, with multiple references to their happy times together in the past.

Everyone was dumbstruck, and the young woman disappeared as quickly as she had arrived. But not before collecting a large fee for her remarkable theatrics, from the quiet Mr. Cole.

69

Put a large note on the rear of a newly married couple's car, saying, "Congratulate these newlyweds, but don't tell them how you know!"

It will drive them crazy, as they stop in gas stations, motels, snack bars, on their trip and are immediately recognized as honeymooners.

70

No chapter on "love" would be complete without a trick from Nick, the Rob Lowe of high society. Nick had some special calling cards printed with his name and phone number. Underneath in big letters, it read "Smile if you'd like a date." He used to present the card to a prospect, and watch as she'd try to hold back the laughter. It was corny, but Nick has the right kind of charisma to pull it off.

The back of the card was printed "Rip this card in two if you're not interested." The zinger was that it was on untearable paper. Some stationers sell envelopes made of this material. It is easy to recognize because it has strands of fiberglass embedded in it. If you want to emulate Nick's ploy, you could cut the cards from this stock, and type the message on. Good luck!

"A guy who twitches his lips is just another guy with a lip twitch—unless he's Humphrey Bogart."

Sammy Davis, Jr.

The classic movie gangster James Cagney once took a car ride with Humphrey Bogart through the Hollywood Hills. Something about Bogart apparently bothered the fastidious Cagney, for soon afterward Cagney penned these lines:

In this silly town of ours,
One sees all primps and poses,
But movies stars in fancy cars
shouldn't pick their fancy noses!

To me this verse provides a much more convincing explanation of the nickname "Bogie" than merely a contraction of Humphrey's surname. Celebrities, especially movie stars, have always had fun at one another's expense. This chapter describes some of the practical jokes played by, with, and on famous people.

71

The film writer Charles MacArthur had a regular schtick at the Hollywood country club. Whenever he met a new member, MacArthur (who fancied himself as a chess expert) would introduce himself as the chess master Capablanca and invite the newcomer to a friendly game. MacArthur was invariably good enough to beat the victim, and he derived some amusement from impersonating Capablanca, who had been world champion some years earlier.

One day, some acquaintances met MacArthur at the club, and introduced him to a rather plain-looking stranger. MacArthur went into his regular routine, and the stranger freely accepted MacArthur's invitation to a chess match. The newcomer hardly seemed to be putting any effort into the match, glancing at the board for a second, making his move, then turning away to engage the others in animated conversation. Nonetheless, after only half-a-dozen moves MacArthur was losing badly and realized he was totally outclassed—by the real Jose Capablanca, who was in town visiting friends! A mild prank, topped with a great boomerang.

72

The classic hotfoot joke involves placing a match into the welt of a victim's shoe, then secretly lighting it. The resultant combustion and attendant "hotfoot dance" provides a merry surprise for both prankster and victim. The hotfoot is so old that it was a popular form of entertainment back in the Civil War, right up there along with lip-syncing Dolly Parton tunes.

You do, however, need a robust physique to give a hotfoot and avoid the unpleasant retaliation that otherwise follows. Jack Dempsey, considered by many the greatest heavyweight boxer of all time, used to boast that he had given more hotfoots than any man alive.

Big deal! Who's going to stand up to the heavyweight champ of the world and spoil his little joke? ("What are you doing down there on the floor, Jack? Uh, giving me a hotfoot? Go right ahead, Jack! Say he's some kidder, ain't he though? Boy, you'll crack us all up with your wit, Jack! Ow! Ow! Arrgggg!")

73

Robert Benchley, the noted humorist and theater critic of the *New Yorker*, was responsible for several class 2 practical jokes when he was a student at Harvard. The one I like best involved a redistribution of davenports. Benchley essentially acted as the Robin Hood of parlor furniture, stealing from those rich in sofas and giving to those less well blessed. Benchley and a couple of cronies were walking through the Beacon Hill district of Boston, when he was seized with the urge to play a prank.

Benchley knocked on the door of the nearest mansion, and announced to the maid that he was there to collect the davenport. There was a sticky moment when the maid wanted to know which one, but Benchley caught sight of one through the open door, and claimed that was it. The maid obviously assumed that they had some lawful business, and let them take it.

Once outside with the chaise, the cronies wanted to know what to do with their heavy ill-gotten gains. Benchley simply marched them all across the street, rang the bell of another mansion, and told the maid he had the davenport for delivery. The crew set it down inside, and withdrew, chuckling about the zinger that would eventually occur when one society dame visited the other's home.

74

Whatever happened to actor Crispin Glover? He played Michael J. Fox's father in *Back to the Future* and co-starred in *River's Edge*, but ominously seems to have disappeared after he nearly kicked David Letterman's head off. Glover was scheduled as a guest on Letterman's chat show. All talk-show guests are screened for sanity and sobriety before appearing on air, and Glover passed the pre-broadcast scrutiny.

Between the test and the broadcast, however, Glover (no relation to *Lethal Weapon* star Danny Glover, by the way) underwent a Dr. Jeckyl/Mr. Hyde style transformation. He changed clothes into aged hippie gear, put on a hideous wig, and took Letterman totally by surprise. Once on the air Glover departed from the arranged script, and tried to show off his "diseased eyeball" collection.

The Letterman audience, always noted for their great discernment and intellect, started heckling. Glover tried to defend himself, arguing that he was strong and (not having a concrete block handy) aimed a karate kick toward Letterman's famous bullet head to prove the point. The program cut to a commercial, and when it came back, astoundingly Glover was gone. At the time Glover claimed that it was "performance art," but in current interviews on MTV he is trying the "evil twin brother" defense, and tries to make out that it wasn't him at all. Is he trying to gain Letterman's confidence for a repeat appearance? I hope so!

75

Buster Keaton, the great silent film star, was an equally great practical joker all his life. During the filming of his last movie *The Railrodder* Buster was standing by a track as a train went slowly by. Buster correctly guessed that it was coming to a halt. The old ham grabbed a handrail on the caboose as it went by and extended his arm with perfect timing. The effect was exactly as if he had pulled the entire train to a stop. The train was about to go backward and with the characteristic deadpan expression, Buster pulled backward. It now looked as though he was now dragging the 100-ton locomotive down the track.

This brilliant and spontaneous improvisation was captured on another film, *The Making of The Railrodder*, and really shows the inventiveness of this comic genius. In his younger, wilder days, Buster had a changing shack on the beach, the sides of which he could collapse instantly by pulling a rope. He would invite groups of film starlets over for a beach party, set up an audience outside the cabin, and at the right moment pull the rope. Timing was all, and unlike the clothes, Buster was never off.

76

I have always liked the "Hollywood Strength Tester." Not unlike a more brutal version of the panic box described in the chapter on science, the strength tester is used to quieten down boastful or overexuberant wise guys on film sets. It is built and maintained by the special effects boys. The thing looks like a big iron version of a dynamite plunger, but instead of pushing it down, the patsy has to pull it up while a dial on top registers his strength.

What actually happens is that, as soon as you give the contraption a mighty tug, all hell breaks loose! A sharp electric shock jolts through the handle while simultaneously a large bore blank cartridge explodes with a deafening crack. Cold water squirts up into the victim's face, and a wooden plank on a lever biffs him in the seat of the pants. It's guaranteed to quiet down an obnoxious strong man for a week or even longer.

77

The modern artist Christo has been internationally active since the mid-1960s. Like a sort of grand-scale Andy Warhol, Christo is known for his trademark art of draping entire buildings in colorful wrappings. Christo also erected a "Running Fence" across miles of California hillside, and created a 20-foot high exhibit on a football field-sized area in New York's Central Park. It looked like laundry hanging out to dry, and Christo solved the problem of vandalism by paying local thugs to guard it.

Surely his masterstroke though was the pyramid constructed of brightly painted oil drums that he convinced a sheik to sponsor in the Middle East. Christo advertised it as "the Great Mastaba of Arabia." Fiddle around with your pants and pull out your pocket dic's, and you'll learn that a "Mastaba" is an Egyptian tomb type of structure. And of course a "tor" is a hill or mound.

Thus Christo has knowingly or unknowingly (I like to think knowingly) made the powerful Sheik Qaboos the Great Mastaba-tor of the Emirates. Life doesn't get any better than this.

78

When meeting a friend at any Middle East airport, greet them with:

"Mr. Rushdie, it is so good to see you!"

79

At Cornell University, sci-fi author Kurt Vonnegut (then a student) went to a physics class where a professor was handing back graded examination papers. Allegedly Kurt saw his grade, and asked the professor to increase it. The professor refused, and Kurt started to beg him in increasing desperation. When the tutor made a final adamant refusal, Vonnegut gave a histrionic scream, and hurled himself through the open window . . . into a net that his friends were holding below. Zinger: it wasn't his paper—he wasn't even taking the course!

80

After the great classic actor John Barrymore died, his friend Raoul Walsh bribed the mortuary attendent and borrowed the body for a couple of hours. Walsh took it to Errol Flynn's house and set it up in a chair. Errol had been a good drinking buddy of the deceased. He came in, and saw his recently departed chum apparently smoking a cigarette. Not surprisingly, he freaked out.

Barrymore, Flynn, and Walsh all led variously dissolute lives, and this practical joke is perhaps less macabre than it seems. Walsh was genuinely a good friend of Barrymore's, and was with him near the end, when the old ham was wildly suggesting that he be immortalized through the imprint of, not his hand, but his testicles in the cement outside Grauman's Chinese Theater.

81

Paul Newman has something of a reputation as a prankster, as well as a friendly rivalry with Robert Redford. It was entirely natural for Newman to put the two together, when he heard that Redford had just taken delivery of a new red Porsche.

Newman arranged for the real Porsche to disappear from Redford's driveway for a couple of hours, and for a totaled, compacted Porsche of the same shade to be dumped there instead. The diminutive troubadour was not amused when he saw what had apparently happened to his new car while his back was turned.

82

What has 500 legs and 6 teeth? Why, the front row at a Willy Nelson concert, of course. Willy Nelson's wife is said to have sewn him into the bedsheets when he came home drunk one night. She then beat him with a broom until she was satisfied that he got the message. This does provide some sort of inspiration for the problem of dealing with amateur drunkards at college.

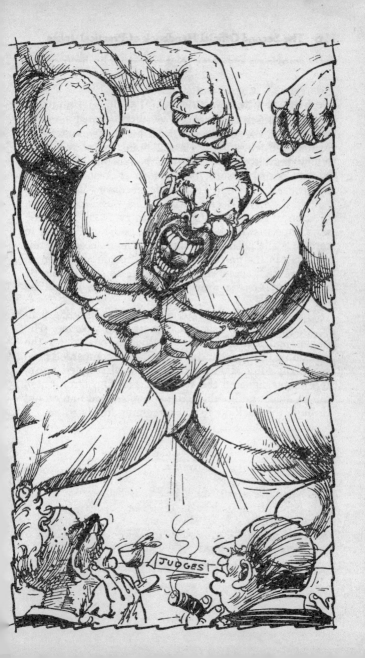

83

In the film *Pumping Iron* the bodybuilder and film star Arnold Schwarzenegger reveals the great sense of humor that shows through in all his subsequent films. Arnold tells of a great class 2 prank he played on a fellow muscle man. The man had come to him for private posing lessons, but as soon as Arnold saw him he realized his pupil lacked the necessary dedication. Arnold therefore decided that a trick was in order . . .

Accordingly the Austrian Oaf (sorry, "Oak") told the poor dupe that the latest fashion in bodybuilding was to scream while posing. He spent two hours coaching this poor sap in the correct vocalization technique ("Ven ze arms are high above ze head, like zo, ze note should be high. Und ven ze arms are low, ze note should be low").

The poor victim entered his next bodybuilding contest, and put the master's training into practice. The judges and audience were totally unprepared for the screaming routine that this contestant accompanied himself with. After about thirty seconds of stunned noise, the judges signaled the stewards, and four strong men ran on stage, grabbed the dupe, and carried him off out through the back door, still screaming lustily.

A master was explaining the nature of the Tao to one of his novices,

"The Tao is embodied in all software—regardless of how insignificant," said the master.

"Is the Tao in a hand-held calculator?" asked the novice. "It is," came the reply.
"Is the Tao in a video game?" continued the novice. "It is even in a video game," said the master.
"And is the Tao in the DOS for a personal computer?"

The master coughed and shifted his position slightly. "The lesson is over for today," he said.

> Geoffrey James
> *"The Tao Of Programming"*

I once had a great idea for a book of computer folklore. Styled after the womens' medical manual *Our Bodies, Ourselves*, I was going to call it *Our Computers, Our Friends*. I discussed the idea with a few colleagues, and quickly found that the title was misinterpreted as *Our Computers Are Friends*, and from there it was but a short step to *Are Computers Our Friends?*, a question that was invariably firmly answered in the negative. I shelved the project, but the lesson of widely perceived computer intimidation stayed with me.

Novice users, slowly gaining computer literacy, often come up with entertaining explanations for their most frustrating experiences. One beginner was having problems operating a program, and turned to another for advice.

Novice 1: "The program said PRESS ANY KEY TO CONTINUE
Novice 2: "So what did you do?"
Novice 1: "I pressed the space bar."
Novice 2: "You fool! It told you to press the ANY key, and you disobeyed! No wonder the screen melted."

It's not nice to play practical jokes on beginners because it is unworthy to harass the already harassed. It's not possible to play practical jokes on the power user or system manager, because they will take away your privileges and disable your account. There is, however, a large class of your competent colleagues who will appreciate you taking the time and trouble to brighten their day with some of these ideas.

84

Fridge magnets are perfect for warping CRT pictures. The small magnetic field deforms the electron beam and makes the picture wavy. Gum the magnet on the side of the terminal to keep it wavy. Many modern terminals have a de-gaussing switch on the back that will instantly restore the squareness of the display. If not, it will probably wear off naturally a few minutes to hours after you remove the magnet. In any case we can deduct the cost of a new terminal from your paycheck.

85

Unpopular managers may not realize it, but they run the risk that programmers will use their technical abilities to redress past wrongs. I heard about one systems programmer who was rudely treated by a manager, demanding special treatment for an ordinary computer job. The next release of the operating system had a special feature, inserted by the programmer. When it recognized jobs with this manager's user ID, a deliberate delay would be inserted after each I/O operation. The amount of delay was initially minuscule, but it increased slightly each week.

The clueless manager's jobs ran imperceptibly slower each week. After several months he found that he could no longer get his precious reports finished in time for them to be of use, so he stopped using the computing facility altogether, which made everybody very happy.

86

A similar, but less vicious prank is to add a time delay to someone's command file executed at log in. Like the preceding modification, have it add a few seconds each day to the delay. When the delay is increased gradually, people adapt to it. See how long you can keep them waiting before they figure it out!

87

In the old Coleco-Vision Smurfs home computer game the object was for the Boy Smurf to run through an assortment of dangers to reach the Girl Smurf. He finally leaps up on the raised platform she is on, grabs her, and they run back through the monsters to get back to the beginning.

If you stop the Boy Smurf from leaping up on the platform at the last moment, however, the Girl Smurf will (presumably to entice him up there) rip off all her clothes! If you own one of these games, you can see this unexpected feature for yourself. Go to the last screen, jump up onto the skull, but turn away before you jump onto the platform. Then jump down from the skull and walk to the edge of the screen. Stop just before you step off the screen. Smurfette closes her eyes and her dress disappears.

No wonder Smurfs have that characteristic blue color.

88

The company where I work carries out most of its internal communication through electronic mail, commonly known as e-mail. This is a very efficient way to conduct business; for example, if you have a payroll query, you can immediately send a note to the payroll department, which they can deal with at their leisure. Sometimes, I find some of these service departments are a little too leisurely in responding to my requests for information. That's why I developed the "automated e-mail reminder." I send the initial query, and if there's no reply in a few days, I send them a standard follow-up.

Have you had the chance to find the information I need yet?
Because of your department's slowness to respond in the past, the computer will automatically repeat this reminder according to the following schedule:
first three days—daily
next two days—every 30 minutes
after that—every minute
Thank you for your attention, and I look forward to your early reply.

It's amazing how they jump to it! The record for holding out is held by one of our accounts departments, and even they managed to get their act together before the e-mail started coming in every thirty minutes. This method has never failed me! The sought-for information always comes back to me within a few days.

What I find really funny though, is the fact that every department subjected to this technique invariably includes with their reply a request (never granted) for a copy of this reminder program. The truth of the matter is that my method works so well that I have never had to bother to create the reminder program. It doesn't exist except in my imagination.

89

If you are prepared to do a little typing, you can prepare a real surprise for a friend's PC. The appendix has the program listing of a replacement COMMAND. COM file. This amusing program was supplied by Tom

Jennings of San Francisco. Type the program in, compile it, and put it on a spare floppy system disk. (Make sure you have another disk with a real COMMAND.COM so you can recover from this.) Then reboot the system using your disk. This program gives you a funny temporary replacement for the PC command interpreter. It responds in strange and insolent ways to all user commands. We've heard about "user-friendly" software for years—this is a breakthrough in user-hostile software.

90

One PC programmer has a special prop that he uses to make fun of people's instincts to keep magnets away from diskettes. He keeps an old-style 5¼ inch floppy disk, labeled "system disk—save!" near his PC at work, stuck to the side of a file cabinet with a small magnet. It really draws stares from newcomers, because it goes against everything they have been warned about.

The zinger comes when they call him on it. He pops it in the drive, reboots, and lists the disk directory. It works! Then he claims to use a special magnet that doesn't affect the disk. Boy, they just don't make residual magnetic fields like they used to. Of course, what's really happening is that the system information (the file allocation table, etc.) on a blank PC disk happens to be on the outside edge of the diskette; he carefully positions the magnet toward the middle of the disk. If you try this for yourself, you'd better experiment first with one of your friend's disks that you can afford to lose.

91

Chad is one of those things that has almost passed into history now, like gas lamps, street horse troughs, and Madonna. Chad is the name for the little pieces of confetti that are punched out of punched cards. With the rise of online systems, fewer and fewer people use punched cards, so the legacy of chad is going too. Play with chad while ye may.

An old college trick was to fill a vacuum cleaner hose with chad, connect it to the "blow" end of the cleaner, and force-feed the chad under someone's office or dormitory door. A special feature is that the movement through the hose caused the chad to become statically charged. It would stick to everything inside the room— walls, ceilings, clothes, windows. It couldn't even be brushed off because the static charge would cause it to jump away from your hand or broom. Yes, chad was certainly entertaining enough. Perhaps this is why they stopped making it.

92

The Apple Macintosh* is a great little computer that popularized many innovations in human interface and user friendliness. An unknown programmer invented a dialogue box for the Macintosh. It would pop up on the screen and offer the alternatives:

```
Sorry, the computer has crashed. To whom would
you like to assign the blame?

    Hardware

    Power Surge

    Sunspots

    Cosmic Rays

    Programmer
```

The PROGRAMMER button was dimmed so you couldn't click on it. . . .

*Macintosh is a trademark of Apple Computer Inc

Everything in the Macintosh world is called "Mac-something," but have you heard about "MacPuke"? It's a small utility program that pops the floppy disk out of the drive, while making a realistic vomiting sound on the loudspeaker. Once this program is found by an engineer, it tends to be put into immediate use, and it spreads like wildfire around an office. Barf-o-rama!

93

Another programmer I worked with had certain hardware skills. He dismantled one of those novelty Christmas cards that plays a carol, and retrieved the piezoelectric melody chip that it contained. He secretly installed it into his boss's keyboard, and connected it to one of the rarely used LEDs. It turns out that the voltage over a lighted LED is enough to drive one of these CMOS chips. Then he amended the system editor, so it turned on the LED when it started and turned it off when it exited. Result: the boss's terminal played continuous Christmas carols whenever he used the editor.

The people in neighboring offices made him remove this after about half an hour. There's only so much "Winter Wonderland" the human mind can stand.

94

A famous 1960s experiment in computer intelligence involved a program that simulated the responses of a psychiatrist talking to a patient. The program, called ELIZA, made a superficial analysis of the text typed at it, and spat back one of a large number of canned responses built into it. The result was an impressive illusion that fooled quite a large number of computer-naive people.

The Free Software Foundation, for reasons best known to themselves, built this psychiatrist dialogue software into their popular GNU editor product. The GNU-emacs editor is given away free, and is available on most Unix systems (Unix is a trademark of ATT). Once you start up GNU-emacs, issue the command "escape-x doctor." You will be able to take part in an interaction like the following:

COMPUTER: "I am the psychotherapist. Please describe your problems."

ME: "I am feeling tired."

COMPUTER: "Why do you say you are feeling tired?"

ME: "I have been working too hard."

COMPUTER: "Is it because of your plans that you say you have been working too hard?"

ME: "No, it is because my house needs cleaning."

COMPUTER: "Is it because your house needs cleaning that you came to me?"

ME: "Why, can you help with that?"

COMPUTER: "Can you elaborate on that?"

ME: "I was wondering how a computer program can help with housework."

COMPUTER: "Does it bother you that a computer program can help with housework?"

ME: "I'd like to see that!"

COMPUTER: "What makes you believe you might want to see that?"

ME: "Eat raw chad, tape-head."

Notice that the computer usually responds with a question designed to get the user to type in more sentences. It makes no attempt to answer questions, because it has no ability to do so.

Nonetheless the program can keep up an impressive conversation with someone who has never seen it before. It makes a good demonstration if you play it right. I once connected it to one of our technical writers, and told him it was an automatic system that would help him develop documentation. He came back into my office after half an hour, and said he didn't want to use it anymore, because it kept bothering him with personal questions!

95

My good friend "Professor" Moriarty started out as a computer operator, working for a supervisor who was both incompetent and interfering. The supervisor would screw up every job he touched, and in the process cause a lot more work for the other employees. After several weeks of correcting the supervisor's mistakes, Moriarty devised a simple way to keep him out of trouble. He wrote a small program that just spun a tape backward and forward and wrote to it at random intervals.

Whenever Moriarty had to take a break he would pause the real work of the department, and start his special job. The supervisor would see the system running, lights blinking, and tapes moving, so everything looked fine. There would never be any console messages or inputs required, so the supervisor never got an opportunity to screw things up. Later, Moriarty would come back from his lunch break, stop the fake job, and resume the real work.

The supervisor inadvertently boomeranged Moriarty, however. Feeling playful one day, Moriarty flipped a switch on the console so that it printed out in base 16 numbers. This made all messages appear completely unintelligible, so Moriarty called the supervisor over, saying, "Hey, take a look at this, there must be something wrong." The supervisor took one look and pressed the "total system reset" before anyone could stop him. Moriarty spent the rest of the afternoon restarting jobs from checkpoints, and restoring the file system from backups.

96

If you can't program these hacks yourself, there's even a commercial business that will sell you the software ready-made. Weirdware, a division of Mainland Machine, a software developer in San Luis Obisbo Calif., markets a $20 practical joke generator it calls PC Prankster. The software consists of ten pranks that the owner can play on unsuspecting friends or enemies.

The pranks were designed to be amusing rather than malicious or destructive. The jokester stores one of the prank files on the intended victim's hard disk or boot disk. Once that's done, the perpetrator can set the joke to go into action after a certain number of keystrokes right in the middle of whatever program the victim is running at the time.

In one joke, the figure of a huge one-eyed monster appears on the screen, blinks and disappears, allowing the program to resume operation unaltered. Other pranks briefly scramble the PC character set, or make the monitor screen appear to be cracking.

97

Does anyone know of the origins of calling the # character a pound sign? Most computer keyboards have a key labeled with the pound sign, but it does not mean that you should pound on the terminal. There is one imaginative use for the pound key on a computer terminal or typewriter, and that is to play a game of ticktacktoe. Use a pen or pencil with a very fine point. Wipe the key clean at the end of each game so the playing field will be clear for the next game.

"Work is the greatest thing in the world, so we should always save some of it for tomorrow."

Don Herald

Did I ever tell you about the time they made me acting manager of an entire 500-person organization? This occurred one Christmas Eve due to the company practice of delegating responsibilities whenever people were absent. On this particular day, people were missing all over the place, and responsibility had been passed up, down, backward, and sideways throughout the organization so much, that the buck finally slid to a halt against my desk. I gleefully seized the buck, and spent it!

The first thing I did on assuming command was to close the building and send everyone home on account of the "Snow Emergency." No, actually that was the second thing I did. The first thing was to use my delegated authority to sign an order authorizing a new carpet and executive desk for my cubicle. After the Christmas holiday a vice president questioned me about closing the plant: "What was this 'snow emergency' "? he wanted to know. "Well," I explained lamely, "there was no emergency." The delegation policy got clarified quite a bit, soon after that. Since most people spend more than half their adult waking hours at work, it's important to find ways to enjoy it. Perhaps some of these ideas will help.

98

Obtain a copy of a magazine that your intended victim wouldn't be caught dead reading. Frederick's lingerie catalog is good for prudes. A wrestling fanzine is just the thing for snooty highbrow types. Forge a mailing label with the victim's name and any plausible address on it. Glue the label to the publication. Place the publication, apparently subscribed to by the nimrod, in the staff lunchroom for co-workers to marvel at. You can't tell which way a train has gone by looking at the tracks, and if you're careful enough, there'll be no way to track you down either.

99

New guys in a factory are typically sent on fool's errands for nonexistent items like a bucket of steam, a skyhook, a left-handed monkey wrench, and so on. A foreman (who should have known better) tried to pull this one on Charlie, when he sent him for a pipe stretcher.

Forty minutes later Charlie drove up to the foreman on the factory's biggest forklift truck. It was loaded down with a gigantic hydraulic contraption, rumbling ominously and belching steam. "Where do you want it, boss?" Charlie inquired innocently. "We're renting it from the hire place at $2,000 a day. I signed it out on your name." That episode brought an immediate end to all the tricks on new guys.

100

If you work in a metal workshop, tack weld a co-worker's lunch pail to the bench. It's funniest of all if he tries to scoop it up as he walks by.

101

A borderline nuisance prank used to be to have something inappropriate sent mail order to a friend's address and let them sort it out. Dirk Wibble O'Dooley, a hot-tempered colleague of mine, received a subscription to a series of porcelain animal thimbles this way.

After months of being threatened with bad credit and lawsuits, Wibble showed me the letter he was sending the manufacturer. He was obviously aiming to impress upon them that his case was not worth pursuing. His note was scrawled in huge block letters with an orange crayon, on the back of a brown paper grocery bag; it read:

DEAR SIRS
I DIDN'T ORDER YOUR STUPID ANIMAL
THIMBLES!
I DON'T EVEN SEW!

SUE ME, BASTARDS!
   DIRK WIBBLE O'DOOLEY

Boomerang! They *did* sue, and Wibble went to a debtor's prison for twelve years. They let him keep the thimbles though, and we all got a good laugh.

102

Most people dislike filling out forms, especially if there is no good reason for it. Some shops have started trying to get your address even when you pay with cash. It then goes on a mailing list, and you'll be bombarded with junk mail for evermore.

When they ask for my address, and I don't think they have any real reason to know it, I sometimes put Address: 1313 Harbor Blvd. Anaheim, CA, which is Disneyland. Phone numbers are equally easy. I use (714) 999-4000, which is Disneyland again.

Nick had the most creative form-filling though. When we were at college together he showed me a midterm exam paper that he had handed to a beautiful teaching assistant proctor whom he wanted to get to know better. It read:

Hi, my	**Name:**	*is Nick. How about*
a	**Date:**	*so I can*
	Score:	*?*

I'll tell you, some days that fellow operates like a well-oiled machine. A *very* well-oiled machine. He did not ace the midterm. He did not get the **Date**. He did not **Score**.

103

It's always a pleasure to visit the dentist's office, so share your joy. First, as you lean back into that leather chair, SCREAM REAL LOUD! Second, do it powerfully enough that all the people still in the waiting room can hear how happy you are! Finally, hope that "Dr. Drillerkiller" has a sense of humor to match yours! When I did this, I obviously made an impression on the dental hygienist for she presented me with a tiny kid's "Sesame Street" toothbrush ("Gonzo" as I recollect) on the way out. Could there be a connection? Surely not.

104

Confound the bureaucrats with fake office memos! The five memos below were all circulated in N.Y. attorney Rudolf Giuliani's (he was then a federal prosecutor) Manhattan office in the summer of 1988. Lawyers are a lot more verbose than this, so I've condensed them down to the interesting parts.

Memo #1: Written by a member of the N.Y. attorney's official memo-writing staff.
To: All Staff
The Summer Office Boat Ride will be on Monday, July 18. Boarding begins at 6:30 P.M. from Pier 62 on 23rd Street.

Memo #2: Written by a member of the N.Y. attorney's official memo-writing staff.

To: All Staff

We are heavily oversubscribed for the summer boat ride and therefore need your help in reducing the number of attendees. If you signed up for the boat ride but now know that you cannot attend, or if you no longer plan to bring a guest, or if, given our oversubscription problem, you generously decide not to bring a guest, please let the committee know. Your cooperation will help us avoid more drastic means of reducing attendance. At the time of boarding, we will have to check attendance, which is limited to those persons who submitted RSVP forms by no later than July 11.

Memo #3: Written by a member of the N.Y. attorney's official memo-writing staff.

To: All Staff

We have not been able to solve our oversubscription problem for the summer boat ride, and unfortunately will have to cut back on the number of guests at the event. We regret that we will only be able to accommodate spouses or "significant others" of staff. Please do not bring as guests anyone but a spouse or "significant other." In addition, using other people's RSVPs as a means of bringing friends on board will not be permitted.

Only those people who submitted RSVP forms by July 11 will be allowed to board the boat. We will be checking attendance that night, so please bring office IDs with you to the boat ride. To avoid embarrassment for yourself or others, please abide by these requests. Thank you for your cooperation in solving this difficult oversubscription problem.

Memo #4: Written by an anonymous parodist in Giuliani's office and circulated as if written by the N.Y. attorney's memo-writing staff.

To: All Staff

Some confusion has apparently arisen concerning the precise meaning of the term "significant other," as expressed in today's previous memorandum about authorized attendees at the boat ride. By "significant other," we mean truly significant others, i.e., persons with whom you have slept within the past month. Lest further confusion arise as a result of this classification, let us go further into defining our terms. By "slept with," we mean sexual relations, including but not limited to sexual intercourse and oral sex.

Only those others who satisfy this definition of "significant" will be allowed to board the boat. To avoid embarrassment for yourself and others, you and your guest should be prepared to respond truthfully to questions concerning the nature and degree of your intimacy. Thank you for your cooperation in solving this difficult oversubscription problem.

Memo #5: Written by N.Y. attorney Rudolf Giuliani himself.

To: All Staff

Apparently the office was circulated today with a memo concerning Monday's boat ride that may have been intended as humor or as a practical joke. It was neither humorous nor a joke. In fact, it was distasteful and upsetting to many.

Everyone in the office can appreciate someone with a sense of humor. I hope that the person who sent this will understand that this message was out of bounds and offensive. It ought not to have been done and under no circumstances is it or anything like it to be repeated. Fair warning.

In the face of such a strict and dire reaction, there's only one thing to do. Follow up with another memo, apparently from Giuliani, castigating the fake Giuliani, and saying he hoped people were not taken in, and realized that he had a better sense of humor than that expressed in the previous memo. Knowledge is power, you shouldn't get into a pissing match with a donkey, and bosses shouldn't fight bogus memos with even more memos.

105

The building where I work has motion sensors wired up to the light switches. This is designed to save energy, by turning the lights on when you enter a room and off again a few minutes after you leave. I've always felt this is a very considerate feature—if you fall asleep at your desk, it turns the lights off!

We engineers soon discovered that there were two adjustments on the sensors: delay and sensitivity. Every few days I would go into the boss's office, and crank these adjustments down by 10 percent. Over a period of weeks, he gradually found that he had to get up more and more often and flap his arms more and more energetically, in order to keep the lights on. For a while he started to believe that his office was possessed by evil spirits. Naturally, I would be all too pleased to conduct an exorcism ceremony ("out, out, foul demons of the Fortran compiler").

106

Get in to work early, and forward all the phones to the desk of one colleague. Remember to forward your own phone too, and don't give yourself away by premature guffaws.

107

Make a photocopy of a really radical picture, something that would embarrass anybody, and put the paper back in the copier paper supply, a couple of dozen sheets down. The chances are that page 3 of the fourth guy's copy will be considerably less boring than all the other pages on all the copies of the memo. This is a pretty good idea, and I'm definitely going to try it this week or next (whichever comes sooner).

108

Embleton was a loathsome oily clerk in my office, and when Michael J. Fox makes his final bow, Embleton will be the vainest man alive. You've heard about giving someone "the straight dope?" Embleton was the straightest dope in the company and I'd been trying to give him away for years. Embleton was more obnoxious than goat farts, and was particularly vain about his luxuriant head of hair. I walked to the elevator lobby one time, brushing past pretty Miss Mimosa who was chatting with someone at the door. Embleton was just around the corner, as usual admiring his hairstyle in the lobby mirror. A cunning plan germinated in my brain, grew, ripened, was harvested, fermented, and ready to serve in the blink of an eye.

"Embleton," I cautioned, "it looks like there may be some kind of huge ugly hairy bug on your back." Cringing coward that he is, Embleton froze solid and begged me to brush it off with my hand. I started gingerly brushing his back until I heard the outer door squeak open. Miss Mimosa was about to arrive! She came through the door, as I reached up with both hands and tugged Embleton's scalp, saying loudly, "I think your toupee is on straight now, Embleton. Just let me know if it slips again. Always pleased to help." Mimosa stared at Embleton, then started giggling. I smiled at Mimosa.

They say that the wicked flee when no one pursueth, and Embleton certainly lit out of there as though his tail were on fire.

109

Many computer facilities have raised floors, which means that you can pull up the floor panels and crawl around underneath where the cables are. This is a simple but unobvious way of passing to the far side of locked doors. Once there, you can construct glitter traps at your leisure.

There is also the (possibly apocryphal) story of a couple of computer engineers who put on miner's hard hats (the ones with the little lights), pulled up a floor panel, and got in under the floor. They tunneled their way to the spot directly beneath the secretaries' word processing area. Then they pushed up a floor panel from below and emerged. That one raised a few eyebrows.

110

The new wonder drug Minoxidol from the Upjohn Corporation is the only known prophylactic that will actually cause new hair to grow. It has to be applied to the scalp several times daily, so users sometimes bring it in to work with them. I sometimes wonder what would happen if you took some of this drug and swapped it for cold cream. I suppose the baldie would stay bald but get greasier, whereas the person with the cold cream would grow hair on their chest.

That's too cruel. I would just change the Minoxidol instructions from "apply to scalp with a swab" to "rub into scalp with palms of hands." In a few weeks your victim will be transformed into a hirsute werewolf. As George Bernard Shaw remarked in *Man and Superman* (his early chronicle on the famous man of steel from the planet Krypton), "do *not* do unto others as you would have them do to you; their tastes may differ from yours."

Book Bedlam
and Library
Lunacy

"La vrai disette, c'est l'absence de livres." (Real poverty is lack of liver.)

Colette

Mark Twain once complained to a clergyman that every word of a sermon he had just preached was in a book in his (Twain's) library. The clergyman was mortified at the thought of unwittingly copying the work of another—until Twain sent the book over. It was a dictionary.

I love all kinds of literary lunacy and, with the regularity of a fruit bat in a plum tree, I mail all my friends really funky postcards. I once sent Wibble a picture postcard of the planet earth, bearing the message: "Wish you were here." His reply? A picture of a prison: "Wish you were here. Wish I wasn't." Going to prison was his own fault for flagrantly ignoring the sign in the library in the tough part of town: "Quit yo' yapping." That, coupled with the "thimble incident" made him a repeat offender. Tough town, tough library. Tough luck, Wibble. Wibble's long life of crime started when he got caught copying an exam in class. The teacher heard the "swish" of the Xerox machine. Here's your chance to "read all about it."

111

Confuse people by inserting some bogus pages full of a foreign language into your favorite book! Wouldn't that be a laugh riot?

Pourquoi les femmes aiment-elles tant monter à cheval? Quoique relativement sportive, monter à cheval ne m'a jamais attirée et longtemps, je me suis demandé de quel attrait secret cette grosse bestiole pouvait se targuer pour que tant de femmes se passionnent pour l'équitation. Je ne manquais donc jamais l'occasion de questionner les cavalières que je rencontrais. Toutefois, leurs réponses me laissaient insatisfaite. Je sentais qu'elles me dissimulaient l'essentiel. Ce n'est qu'il y a trois ans que la vérité m'est enfin apparue.

Madelaine est une excellente copine, jeune modèle occasionnelle, que j'ai rencontrée l'année dernière. Le seul plaisir que nous ne partagions pas était sa passion pour le cheval. Elle ne pouvait s'en passer et chaque jour elle m'abandonnait une heure pour galoper sur son hongre à travers la campagne.

Un après-midi, tandis qu'elle partait pour sa promenade habituelle, je décidai d'aller à pied jusqu'au village faire nos courses. Au retour, pour fuir la route que le soleil avait transformée en fournaise, je me suis risquée à emprunter un sentier de traverse. Seulement, je connaissais encore mal la région, et d'embranchement en embranchement, et à force de contourner les haies, je finis par m'égarer.

Cela n'avait rien de dramatique et je venais de prendre le parti de m'orienter sur le soleil lorsque j'aperçus le cheval de Madelaine en train de brouter. J'entendis un cri. Il venait de ma droite. J'ai tourné la tête et là, à moins de cinq mètres, à peine dissimulée par un maigre buisson, il y avait mon amie, debout, intégralement nue, les jambes largement écartées, et se branlant d'une main agile, tandis que, de l'autre, elle se fouettait savamment la chatte, l'intérieur des cuisses, les seins, et même le visage avec sa cravache. Ses traits avaient une lubricité sans limites.

"C'est plus fort que moi", m'a-t-elle répondu en retrouvant lentement son calme. "Mais parfois, le frottement de ma chatte sur le pommeau de la selle finit par me faire perdre la tête. Je deviens lubrique. Des idée cochonnes m'assaillent. Alors . . ."

Un long silence avait suivi ses premières confessions.

Agenouillées face à face, elle, nue et les mains posées au creux de ses cuisses largement ouvertes et moi, jouant distraitement avec la cravache que je n'avais pu me retenir de ramasser, nous étions à nous regarder sans plus savoir quoi nous dire. Nos coeurs battaient la chamade. Et puis, subitement, cela a éclaté. Mue par une force irrésistible, j'ai glissé la cravache à l'intérieur de ses cuisses et je l'ai poussée vers sa chatte. Dans un râle sourd, elle s'est effondrée dans l'herbe.

Ainsi, c'était ça! Enfin, je l'avais, ma réponse. Mais sur l'instant, je n'en avais cure. Nous étions dépassées par nos instincts.

Madelaine est une excellente copine, jeune modèle occasionnelle, que j'ai rencontrée l'année dernière. Le seul plaisir que nous ne partagions pas était sa passion pour le cheval. Elle ne pouvait s'en passer et chaque jour elle m'abandonnait une heure pour galoper sur son hongre à travers la campagne.

Un après-midi, tandis qu'elle partait pour sa promenade habituelle, je décidai d'aller à pied jusqu'au village faire nos courses. Au retour, pour fuir la route que le soleil avait transformée en fournaise, je me suis risquée à emprunter un sentier de traverse. Seulement, je connaissais encore mal la région, et d'embranchement en embranchement, et à force de contourner les haies, je finis par m'égarer.

Cela n'avait rien de dramatique et je venais de prendre le parti de m'orienter sur le soleil lorsque j'aperçus le cheval de Madelaine en train de brouter. J'entendis un cri. Il venait de ma droite. J'ai tourné la tête et là, à moins de cinq mètres, à peine dissimulée par un maigre buisson, il y avait mon amie, debout, intégralement nue, les jambes largement écartées, et se branlant d'une main agile, tandis que, de l'autre, elle se fouettait savamment la chatte, l'intérieur des cuisses, les seins, et même le visage avec sa cravache. Ses traits avaient une lubricité sans limites.

"C'est plus fort que moi", m'a-t-elle répondu en retrouvant lentement son calme. "Mais parfois, le frottement de ma chatte sur le pommeau de la selle finit par me faire perdre la tête. Je deviens lubrique.

Well, maybe it wouldn't be such a laugh riot, after all.

112

Test the "purity quotient" of your friends and family by opening this book to the title page marked "The Illustrated Book of Nude Photography" and leaving it lying around. If you time this right you can burst into the room just as they've picked up the fateful tome, but before discovering the fraud.

You gain substantial extra points if the embarrassed party whips the book behind his or her back in an attempt to conceal it from you.

113

I wanted to have some pages in this book printed with special nondrying ink that would smear all over your hands as you read them. Unfortunately the publishers wouldn't go for it. I suppose they're right. For surely it is written (for surely you are reading it) that some pranks belong to the class of "impractical jokes." They sound like fun, but take so much setting up that the joke is really on you.

114

But those pages of French allow for even more fun. Persuade a wimp acquaintance to approach a French speaker and translate it. It's a mildly racy story (courtesy of my film-star friend Ian in Paris). Photocopy the page first and use typist correction fluid to white out the book title. Then give it to your prudish friend and ask him to get the new French secretary to put it into English.

115

Official Addendum to the *Scrabble Dictionary*.

These words were inadvertently left out of the *Scrabble Dictionary*. They will give you a real advantage if you know them, because other players will not.

Lynx, quiz, bilj, qrzy, dingleberry, puffin, meson, snit, dork, dirs, thermodynamics, flob, snotty, aardvark, jiz, quux, orgy, splik, wango, fymp, tup, stiq, grok, sleaz, norville, foo, rooney, glum, xyzzy, apogee, throb, klit, quango, floj, barfbag, jomo, xopen, klemper, grazyna, pneumonoultramicroscopicsilicovolcanoconiosises, pushd, penia, ctenoid, kiwi, yremp, yomp, schlong, schmedium, eatmyschorts, gazzle, mo'fo', yeller, quayle, quaaludes.

Produce a photocopy of this page to prove your point.

116

Go and look up *Books In Print* at any bookstore; it's a massive multivolume work, indexed by author name. You can easily find several books written by someone with the exact same name as you.

Buy them, and adorn your office or study with "your" books! For example, I always thought that my surname was pretty unusual, but there is a whole page of "van der Linden," including three different authors also sharing my name! I selected "Squatter Settlements in Karachi," which is strange and obscure enough for even me.

Buy several copies of the work and give them to your friends as Christmas presents. You can even autograph them for added amusement. When disbelievers comment on your hitherto-unknown literary talents, intone a meaningful hollow laugh and point out that you have many talents that you have not yet revealed.

117

One group of students loaded several balloons each with a handful of paper confetti, then filled the balloons with helium. They let these balloons loose in the school's library. The balloons would float around on the ceiling and eventually bump into a light. Upon getting too warm, the balloons would pop and shower floor, books, students, and irate librarians with paper. The climax can be artificially hastened with a pocket catapult.

118

Have you seen the "Aenigmatorum liber Latinorum"? They call it this on the title page, but pathetically wimped out on the cover, where it's identified as *The Latin Riddle Book* by Louis Phillips and Stan Shechter, (published by Harmony Books, 1988, ISBN 0-517-56975-2).

It's a novel book, full of riddles in Latin, such as

Q. Quid gignatur ex hyaena et psittaco?
A. Animal viribus ridendi in ioca sua eximium!

Luckily, English translations are supplied, so we know that the preceding is: What do you get if you cross a parrot with a hyena? An animal that laughs at its own jokes. Yeah, like the authors of that fabulous tome.

My Latin scholarship started with

Caesar adsum jam forti,
    Brutus et erat:
Caesar sic in omnibus,
    Brutus sic in hat.
                    (Anon)

And sadly ended with "Quantum est ille canis in fenestra?" ("How much is that doggie in the window?")

119

Order any of these frightful books and annoy/embarrass/astound/enlighten/delight librarians, or simply mail them as a gift to distant friends:

The book *Fuck Yes*, by Wing F. Fing (published by Shepherd Books, 1988, ISBN 0-940183-21-8).

Tee A. Corinne's literary masterpiece is the *Cunt Coloring Book* (published by Last Gasp, 2180 Bryant St., San Francisco, CA 94110, 1988, ISBN 0-86719-371-9). This book is exactly what the title suggests. The foreword reads, "First published in 1975, the book was immediately and wildly popular, although many people complained about the 'awful' title." Three printings later in 1981, the title was changed to *Labiaflowers* and the book virtually died. So much for euphemisms." Umm, Tee, I don't know how to break this to you . . . but obviously many purchasers of your fine book are folk with a mischievous bent who want to astonish friends and discomfit relations long distance! They *need* that "awful title."

I sent this book to Nick under plain cover the week his ma was staying with him. She eagerly took the parcel from the mailman, and seemed most disappointed when Nick was strangely loath to open it. I'll always be indebted to Nick for pointing out that my name "Peter" is the French for "to fart."

How to Shit in the Woods (published by Ten Speed Press, 1989, ISBN 0-89815-319-0). Let your true feelings be known in this oh-so-subtle way.

Fucking Animals—A Book of Poems by Edmund Miller (published by Edmund Miller, 1973, ISBN 0-9600486-2-6). Complaint against man's fellow creatures, or a must for all animal lovers? You be the judge.

The International Dictionary of Obscenities (published by Scythian Books, 1981, ISBN 0-933884-18-4). Try to get the illustrated edition; it's so much more entertaining.

There are more titles, but that's all I can stand at present. Send your maiden aunt or sister to buy them, or just place them unobstrusively in the boss's bookshelf when you go over for dinner.

120

Hollow out some large books and mount cheap alarm clocks inside the cavity. Set the alarms, and place the books in separate locations in the study area of a library.

It's hilarious to watch Marianne-the-librarian running about trying to figure it all out. The error in the synchronization of the clocks is an added bonus, because each tends to go off about the time the previous one is found. This joke works equally well to relieve the tension in an examination hall.

121

At one college there was an annual "book tear" when students would bring books into the library and put them on the library shelves. At a cue, perhaps the ringing of a class-passing bell, all of the students in the library get up from their studies, pick their own books off the shelves, and rip pages out. They lost several librarians that way.

122

Here's an even better school library prank. Starting about ten days before the library closes at the end of the school year, each day one-tenth of the student body goes to the library and each student checks out as many books as he or she is allowed to. Then, on the last day of term, the entire student body returns their books.

Depending on how many pranksters you can coordinate, you can empty a single shelf, a bookcase, or an entire room of books. This prank has also been known to cause nervous breakdowns in distraught librarians.

123

Has anyone seen an example of the "bogus butterfly"? This is a construction of paper, wire, and a rubber band, that is placed between the pages of a book. When the book is opened, the band unwinds, flaps the paper, and takes off up into the air.

It is an extremely effective surprise, and works well in churches. Plant the bogus butterfly in the Bible on the preacher's lectern. Unfortunately, the secrets of constructions are not known to me. Perhaps some mechanical engineer out there can deduce out how to build, or even where to buy one of these valuable and laff-provoking artifacts?

Count
Dracula

Freaky Phone Stuff

"This 'telephone' has too many shortcomings to be seriously considered as a means of communication. The device is of no value to us."

Western Union memo, 1877

The telephone has evolved rapidly over the past few years. No longer do we just have the plain old telephone service familiar to the older generation. Over the last few years, a bewildering and lucrative (for the phone company) variety of additional phone services has become available. There is:

Call forwarding—when you are expecting a call at home, but you have to go out, you can forward your calls to another number. This can be the place you are going to, or the number of someone who can take a message for you.

Call waiting—this allows you to take a second call that comes in when you are already on the phone. You can flip between the two calls or devote yourself to the more important one. The two people you are talking to can't hear each other. For that you need,

Three-way calling—this feature makes it possible for you to talk to two parties at once, making a total of three parties on the line.

Caller ID—when your phone rings, a little display panel by your phone lights up with the number that is calling you. In theory this allows you to distinguish between your brother-in-law and a sales solicitor and avoid either or both.

Cellular phones—these are walkie-talkies that talk to one of several base stations connected to the phone network. The radio interface has been made fully automatic, so the end you hold in your hand acts exactly as a normal phone. A cellular phone may be installed in a car or boat, or even fitted with self-contained batteries to be fully portable. A cellular phone can be used anywhere within range of a base station, typically covering an entire city. A cordless phone works the same way, but there is only one base station, and the range is just a few dozen yards.

Special numbers—When you call an 800 number, the call is free to you but is billed to the owner of the line. When you call a 900 number, there is a surcharge, typically several dollars per minute, that is added to your bill by the phone company and paid over to the owner of the line; 900 numbers are widely used by adult chat hot lines.

Phones now come with more features and options than you find in a new car. With each of these new developments, the opportunities for practical jokes has also grown.

124

Find two pay phones (or just two adjacent phones in an office) and call a friend who has the call-waiting feature. When he answers, start dialing his number on the other phone. With call waiting he will correctly think that he has got another call. But when he switches lines, he will find himself still talking to you!

You can try to make him think that there are two different versions of you (one of whom must be an imposter—practice your "evil twin" excuse!) or you can convince him that his expensive call-waiting feature must be broken, and he is perhaps *missing valuable urgent calls, even as you speak!* If you do this right, you can repeatedly call him on the other line and drive him crazy. It is the victim's own fault for letting the telephone rule his life.

125

Unlatch and partially remove the curly cord where it enters the phone handset. When the patsy picks up the phone, the cord flies out and you get to watch him panic trying to plug it back in. Unplugging works very well on technophobes, and you can add to the excitement by waving your arms frantically and shouting an animated warning about the "dial-tone fluid" leaking out of the socket.

126

I once forwarded my phone to a 900 adult service as a joke. Anyone calling my number actually got "Candy's Red Hot Chat-line." I didn't leave it like this for too long, because those 900 numbers really run up the charges. You can achieve some mystifying results this way if you are expecting a call. Your phone line, or that of a colleague, can usefully be forwarded to many other destinations: the Paula Abdul Hot Line, Penn State Football Update, NBC Soap Line, or the speaking clock. I am passing this information on, so that you, too, may warp the minds of the young and impressionable.

127

When I explained some of the new phone features to Harris and Nick, each of them tried to turn it to his own advantage. Nick immediately got an 800 number installed as his home phone; he had it printed on his card, and invites girls to call him free of charge! The snapperhead! Whatever next? "Operators are standing by," I suppose. If dating were made into an Olympic sport, Nick would be major contender in the heavyweight class.

Harris pursues Mammon rather than Madonna and, when he found out about these phone features, he talked excitedly about getting a 900 number! Then you'd pay to call him. As Harris explained, "Time is money, and time flies when you're having fun. Therefore money flies when you're having fun. Have fun!"

128

One engineer used to work on a telephone testing switchboard that had a special test number only ever used by prearrangement. If this phone rang unexpectedly, it was guaranteed to be a wrong number. If this happened on a slow day, the engineer would answer with, "Hello, Midtown wrong numbers, can I help you?" The conversation would then proceed,

Caller: "Umm, who are you?"
Engineer: "Midtown wrong number department"
Caller: "What do you do?
Engineer: "Whenever someone dials a wrong number, we answer it and put them right"
Caller: "Oh . . . Thank you . . ."

and they would hang up. You've got to wonder how long it would take before they found a flaw in the logic of what happened.

129

An easy and harmless gag is to sabotage the microphone portion of a telephone receiver. This works on a standard "desk" phone, or other phone that has the type of handset with the screw-on caps. Unscrew the lower cap, remove the microphone, and put Scotch tape over the contacts. When the mark answers the phone, he will be able to hear the calling party, but the caller won't be able to hear him.

130

Portable phones are still comparatively rare, which means that people have not yet had a chance to get used to them. If you get the opportunity to use a portable phone, here are the gags that go along with it.

- While sitting in a restaurant with lousy service, call up the manager and complain. ("This is table 11, we haven't seen our waiter in twenty minutes!")
- If the service is really slow, call and have a takeout meal delivered to your table from a rival restaurant.
- Call up the grocery store and ask where they hid something. ("I'm standing on aisle 12, and I tell you the sugar isn't there!")
- Order a pizza and tell them to deliver it to your car immediately outside.
- Stand outside a friend's house, and dial their number. After a slight pause, ring the doorbell. Try to predict whether they will answer the door or the phone first. If they get the phone, then advise them that the door is more urgent, and hang up. If they get the door, then hide the phone behind your back, and when they answer it tell them they should have got the phone first.

131

I like to record the message on my answering machine as follows (hurried, frantic tone): "Uh— yeah hello—look, can you hold a minute, the thing's about to—just hold okay?" Keep them waiting for about half a minute while providing an entertaining variety of thumps, bangs, gasps, roars, and such. Then come back on the line: "Sorry, I had to go right out—but you can leave a message after the tone." Most people won't realize that they have been waiting on the convenience of a machine until this point!

132

A great phone trick is answering machine message capture. Call someone interesting and record their answering machine message onto your machine. This ploy allowed me to have the Pope taking phone messages for me! You can do it too.

For the price of an overseas phone call you can access the Vatican's voice mail system and hear a recorded message from Pope John Paul II himself. Vatican Radio uses the system to broadcast daily messages recorded by the Pope in English, Italian, and Spanish. To access the English language service from the United States, dial 011-39-7779-3020. Have a tape recorder handy to record the infallible wisdom, for later editing and insertion onto your answering machine outgoing message.

Message capture also allows you to record the messages from two answering machines onto the other. The confused owners will come home and find that their machines have apparently called each other! A great class 3 practical joke!

133

You can also take the receiver from a phone apart and grate garlic on the inside of the transmitter cover. Have several people call and say something to the effect of "Wow, do you ever stink. What have you been eating?"

134

Never waste a wrong number! If you get repeatedly bothered with calls for "Jackie" that are obviously wrong numbers, ask who's calling. Cover the mouthpiece, then come back after a minute and tell them "Jackie is really furious with you, and doesn't want you to call ever again." Then hang up!

135

A friend was in a department store one day when someone called the time and forwarded it to the paging number so that all through the store the soothing voice could be heard to say, "The time is—and—seconds,

The time is—" It went on for 5 or 6 minutes. A friendly salesman explained that it was done from outside by hackers calling and somehow signaling the electronic switchboard. He went on to say that "time" was rather mild. A week earlier they had used one of those 900 "adult" numbers. I would have liked to have heard that. They had to throw the circuit breaker to the switchboard to kill it.

I believe it's far more likely to have been an inside job. Someone inside the store called the time, and then forwarded it to the extension the PA was on. Of course, blaming "outside hackers" is good policy to divert suspicion from fun-loving sales clerks. Incidentally, did you know that the phone number for the speaking clock in San Francisco is "POP-CORN" (767-2676, although 767-XXXX works)? Appropriately enough, in Boston it's "NERVOUS" (637-8687, although 637-XXXX works).

Wild Life
in the
Fast Lane

"The more you drive, the dumber you get"
Popular folk wisdom

George Carlin once remarked that he'd always wanted to attach four white canes with red tips to the fenders of his car and drive around wearing a pair of dark sunglasses. That may be so, but *my* ideal car would be one of those humungo-bodied jacked-up four-wheel-drive vehicles with a tank engine (Blazer, Bronco, Waggoneer, etc.). It's every American's duty to own, consume, or destroy, and with one of those babies I can do all three at once.

Cars seem to be very personal status symbols to a lot of people. I think it's because so many young mothers and fathers first "conceived" the notion of their children while in the backseat of their own parents' car, and in this way auto-eroticism is passed down from generation to generation. So why not get the biggest vehicle possible and drive your gonads? Speaking of which, Nick used to impress the impressionable by talking about his "Vette" occasionally. Listeners were sometimes disappointed however when they found out it was a CHE-vette and not a COR-vette. When you're out of gas, try some of the auto suggestions in this chapter.

136

I always keep a spare parking ticket in the car. When I need to park in someplace stupid, I slap it on the windshield. Most meter maids don't bother ticketing a car that's already ticketed. But for those awkward buggers that will, or for parking in a really stupid place, I also strew the front seat with recent copies of *Police News* and *Police Gazette*.

This ploy is basically a crock of frog brains, and I certainly met my match with one meter maid. When I returned to my car after using this trick, there were two real tickets propped up next to my fake one. "Well," I commented after thoughtfully considering all sides of the matter, "that certainly sucks the big one."

137

The car enthusiast's magazine *Road and Track* used to have a hilarious policy of testing outlandish vehicles every year in their April issue. I mean *really* outlandish vehicles. In past years they have tested the Oscar Meyer Weinermobile, a railway locomotive, a Mercedes-Benz garbage truck, and fairground bumper cars. They also did comparison testing of Concorde against the *Queen Elizabeth II* ocean liner, and a hot air balloon against the Goodyear blimp.

They treat these spoofs exactly as one of their regular road tests, and duly note the performance characteristics of each vehicle. They supply figures representing the results of acceleration, braking, and maneuverability tests. When testing the *QE2* against Concorde, the tester noted "the *QE2* offers more meals, and the ship's lounges stock 51 brands of whiskey." In the case of the locomotive, the tester couldn't resist pointing out that "this vehicle handles like it's on rails." For the hot-air balloon, under "unladen weight" they had 0 lbs! Unfortunately the editorship of the magazine changed in 1989, and they appear to have dropped this widely appreciated annual feature.

138

One amateur mechanic wired up the brake lights in his dad's car so that when the brakes came on, the horn sounded. That'll teach Dad not to loan junior the car. The next time Dad pulls up at a stop sign, he blasts the car ahead! The car ahead naturally assumes Dad is being impatient, and turns around to glare at him. Dad assumes the car ahead is parking instead of going, and really does blow the horn. Well, you can see where this starts to lead.

139

This old prank was probably first tried on model-T Fords. Lever off a hubcap. Place four or five steel ball bearings into it. Replace the hubcap. When the car is driven, the wheel makes a rattling sound until centrifugal force holds the marbles at the rim. The startled driver will hear a noise like nails rattling in a rusty can, when stopping or starting the car. A real belly-splitter, eh?

140

You know, you can really spook a driver who is trying hard to maneuver into a limited space. As a passenger in the car, all you do is dangle your hand inconspicuously out of the open window. At an appropriate moment, slam your hand against the side of the car. It sounds most realistic. It works well on narrow streets with parked cars, too. You get extra points if your guilty driver takes off in a hurry.

141

The following reports of unofficial road sign changes have reached me:

• On an Indian reservation, a PEDESTRIANS sign consisting of a silhouette of a person walking across a road. Someone had added a headband and feather to the pedestrian.

- A bicycle's red reflector glued on the nose of a deer in the DEER CROSSING sign. Rudolf lives!
- On a sign by a horse trail, there's a silhouette showing a person on a horse. Someone extended the horse's ears and now the proud equestrian is mounted on a donkey.
- Another slightly modified version of a deer crossing. Someone had penciled in another deer mating with the first. This is great because the real deer is leaping—if you paint in the doe underneath it's indistinguishable from the mating position.
- On one of those "crossed knife and fork" signs they use to advertise food services on roadside signs, someone painted in a skull above. From a little way back it resembles a skull and crossbones and in many cases is a much more accurate foretaste of the culinary services.

142

The wonderfully dangerous sport of Winnebago Surfing was invented by rock climbers in a national park in the western United States. The surfer lurks in an overhanging tree, rock, or output port of a tunnel, and hops a ride on the top of a slow-moving motor home driven by a tourist.

The successful auto-surfer then waves at passing motorists, jumps up and down noisily on the roof, or hangs upside-down over the windshield and makes faces at the driver (while anchored securely with climbing equipment, since the panicking driver invariably hits the brakes)! Ideally, the surfer catches another tree or pre-rigged rope and disappears vertically before the old-timer (Winnebago's are usually driven by those in their golden years) can dismount to investigate.

Phew! Is anybody actually demented enough to do this, or is it just another fabulous urban legend? An informant in the National Park Service says that the Department of the Interior ordered rangers to deal

harshly with Winnebago surfers, and to suppress all mention of Winnebago surfing in internal newsletters and publications, lest the practice become widespread. Har Har HAR—TOO LATE!

143

In a crowded parking lot, wave your keys around and pretend to be heading to your car. People looking for a parking spot follow you all over the place. Cut through the space between two cars and enjoy watching them go crazy trying to race up to the end of the row and down the next one to follow you.

144

The Revenger is a portable noise generator that fits in a car and lets the frustrated driver vent aggressive impulses. The instrument, which looks like a radar detector and attaches to your vehicle's dashboard, contains a sound chip and a row of lights. When the Revenger is turned on, the lights start flashing, and the driver has the option of pressing three buttons: machine-gun (rat-a-tat-tat), grenade launcher (a whistle and a boom), or a death ray (a high-pitched oscillating frequency). A typical use of the death-ray sound effect would be to discourage pedestrians from jaywalking. In a February 1989 column, Ann Landers railed against the Revenger, asking, "Where is the agency that polices these 'toys'? Here's something it ought to look into." With a denunciation like that, you know it's got to be good!

I have one of these, but I don't use it in the car. I use it while following people out of shops that have shoplifting detector gear. The shop assistants hear the high-pitched oscillating tone, and recognize that it is not the alarm, but the victim doesn't know that. The best time was when someone (obviously with a guilty conscience) made a run for it! Do not do this at an airport security check, unless you want to spend several years sharing a windowless 8 by 8 room with Charles Manson.

145

Remember the way warplanes used to stencil silhouettes of their "kills" on the side of the cockpit? I have seen a car driving around with silhouettes of bicycles, assorted animals, children, and so on, plastered on the side of the driver's door.

That suggests a challenging variant. If this isn't a decoration you want for your own car, then make a gift of it to a deserving neighbor (use the passenger door to avoid early discovery). This reminds me of the sticker I once saw on a big rig. It read "This truck is driven by a professional. His driving kills are on display." I don't know if the first "s" from "skills" was dropped deliberately, but the phrase certainly made a whole lot more sense in its amended form.

Epilog

The author invites readers to send in descriptions of their own favorite practical jokes. The first sender of each prank selected for inclusion in a future volume will receive a free copy of that edition, together with a full acknowledgment therein.

Pranks will be judged on:

humorous content

originality

legibility of your handwriting

how I'm feeling that day

Send your pranks, with a self-addressed stamped envelope, to:

Peter van der Linden,
c/o NAL Penguin Inc,
375 Hudson Street
New York,
NY 10014.

And remember, you can never have too much fun!

Appendix:
The Happy
Hacker

There have been many news stories over the past year or two about computer viruses. Many people wonder what they are exactly. The industry now recognizes these nuisances:

- Worm—a program that moves from workstation to workstation. There is usually one copy per machine, RAM resident, and it propagates itself via a network.
- Trojan horse—a program that performs some apparently useful function, but also contains hidden instructions that perform an unwanted malicious function. It is file resident, and is planted by malevolent human beings.
- Bacterium—a program that replicates itself without bound, thereby preempting the resources of the host system. There will be many self-propagating copies per machine.
- Virus—a program that incorporates copies of itself ("infects") into the machine code of other programs, and when those programs are invoked, performs a malicious function. Often propagated through infecting the startup code on a disk.

These are undesirable for two reasons. First, they are simply destructive. Second, they take place outside the control of the perpetrator. It is not possible simply to stop one of these once it is released. The computer industry, and the federal authorities, quite rightly deal harshly with people who generate these kinds of nuisances. If you are ever tempted to try one of these, don't. They go way outside the acceptable bounds of a prank. I only mention them here (without any technical details of their construction) to warn readers not to have anything to do with this kind of nuisance.

In contrast to the unacceptable practices described previously, it can be amusing to fool a PC user by making him think the PC is talking back. This can be done by typing in the program below and using it as a joke temporary replacement for the PC command interpreter. The program responds in strange and insolent ways to all user commands. Think of it as a breakthrough in user-hostile software.

Make certain that you keep an original copy of the file COMMAND.COM so that you can re-boot and get back to normal. Then compile this C program, save it as COMMAND.COM., and boot the PC from the disk with it on.

```c
#include <stdio.h>
#include <ctype.h>
/*  A replacement for COMMAND.COM   */
version = 0;
char drive = 'A';
unsigned rnd;                    /* pseudo random number */

#define same (s1,s2)  (strcmp(s1,s2)  = = 0)

main () {
long l;
char ln[132];
char cmd[80],*arg,*cp;

        for (l= 10000L; l > 0L; l--);        /* look busy */

        cprintf("Current date is Tue   1-01-1980\r\n");
        get(ln,"Enter New date: ");
        cprintf ("Current time is 0:01:21.32\r\n");
        get(ln,"Enter new time: ");

        cprintf("\r\n\r\nThe IBM Personal Computer DOS\r\n");
        cprintf("Version 2.00 (C)Copywrong IBN Corp 1981,
1982, 1983\r\n");

/* Now the fun starts */

        drive = 'A';
        while (1)  {
          cprintf("%c>",drive);
          drive + = 7; if (drive > 'Z') drive = 'A';
          get(ln," ");        /* get command line */
          arg= cmd;           /* copy of command name */
          cp= ln;
          while (*cp && (*cp != ' '))
                        *arg+ + = *cp+ +;
```

```
        *arg= '\0';          /* terminate cmd name */
        while (*cp && (*cp = = ' '))   /* skip spaces, etc */
                        + +cp;
        arg= cp;              /* arg is cmd tail */

        if (same(cmd, "dir")) dir ();
        else if (same(cmd,"ver")) ver();
        else if (same(cmd,"cd")) cd(arg);
        else if (same(cmd,"chdir")) cd(arg);
        else if (same(cmd,"date")) date(arg);
        else if (same(cmd,"time")) time(arg);
        else if (same(cmd,"ren")) del(arg);
        else if (same(cmd,"del")) del(arg);
        else if (same(cmd,"erase")) del(arg);
        else if (same(cmd,"prompt")) prompt(arg);
        else if (same(cmd,"set")) set (arg);
        else if (same(cmd,"exit")) exitc();
        else if (strlen(cmd) > 0) command(cmd,arg);
    }
}
/* Display wrong MSDOS version */
ver() {
    version + = 137;
    cprintf("IBM Personal Computer DOS version
        2.%d\r\n",version);
    cprintf("\r\n");
}
/* DOS prompt */
prompt() {
    cprintf("But I like the prompt as it is\r\n");
    cprintf("\r\n");
}
/* set environment */
set(s)
char *s;
{
    if (strlen(s)) cprintf("%s? ",s);
    cprintf("That sounds interesting\r\n");
    cprintf("\r\n");
}
/* Exit program */
exitc() {

    cprintf("No, I am not going away.\r\n");
```

```c
    cprintf("\r\n");
}
/* delete some files */
del() {
    disk(); disk();

    if (chance(50)) dosmsg();
    else cprintf("File not found\r\n");
    cprintf("\r\n");
}
/* dont list disk files */
dir() {

    if (chance(30)) dosmsg();
    else {
       disk();
       cprintf("Volume in drive %c: label fell off\r\n", drive);
       disk(); disk();
       cprintf("Directory of %c:\\\r\n",drive);
       cprintf("\r\nFile not frammished\r\n");
    }
    cprintf("\r\n");
}

/* Refuse to change directories */
cd(arg)
char *arg;
{
    if (chance(40) dosmsg();
    else cprintf("Invalid directory\r\n");
    cprint("\r\n");
}
/* Set the time */

time() {
    if (chance(35)) cprintf("Time? Who has time?\r\n");
    else if (chance(15)) cprintf("I forget\r\n");
    else cprintf("Buy a watch\r\n");
    cprintf("\r\n");
}

/* Set the date */

date() {
    if (chance(25)) cprintf("My birthday!\r\n");
```

```
    else if (chance(25)) cprintf("Most banks give out calendars,
      get one\r\n");
    else cprintf("Sometime after 1980\r\n");
    cprintf("\r\n");
}

/* Display a prompt, input a line of text, convert it to all
lower case. While we're at it, generate a fake random number
by continually incrementing an integer while waiting for a
key. */
get(1,p)
char 1[];
char *p;
{
int i,j;
char c;
    cprintf ("%s",p);
    i = 0
    while (1)   {
        while (! (c= bdos(6,0xff))) rnd + = 17;
/* Backspace and delete: MOST of the time, do it right. Once
in a while, backspace by deleting the whole line, and restor-
ing it all except the last deleted character. */
        if ((c = = 8) | | (c = = 127))   {
            if (i > 0)   {
                if (chance(30))   {
                    for (j= i; j--;) cprintf("\010 \010");
                        --i;
                    for (j= 0; j < i; j+ +) bdos(6,1[j]);
                } else {
                        --i;
                        cprintf("\010 \010");
                }
            }
/* control-c probably means banging on the keyboard in frus-
tration */
        } else if (c = = 3)   {
            switch (rnd % 4)   {
            case 0: cprintf("Ouch!\07\r\n"); break;
            case 1: cprintf("Cut it out!\r\n"); break;
            case 2: cprintf ("Stop it!\r\n"); break;
            case 3: cprintf("That hurts!\r\n"); break;
            }
            i= 0;
            break;
```

*   *   *

```
/* Carriage return; be merciful */

        } else if (c = = 13)  {
             cprintf("\r\n");
             break;

/* Tabs are fun. Space over a random number of spaces */

        } else if (c = = 9)  {
             for (j= (rnd % 6) + 4; j > 0; --j)  {
                  bdos(6,' ');
                  l[i++]= ' ';
             }
/* Control characters: normal until I figure out what to do */
        } else if (c < ' ')  {
             cprintf("^%c",c + '@');

        } else {
             bdos(6,c);
             l[i++]= c;
        }
    }

    l[i]= '\0';
    for (i= 0; l[i]; i++) l[i]= tolower(l[i]);
}
/* Chance: the number given is a percentage of 100, return
true if we are in range.   */
chance(n)
int n;
{
    return(n > (rnd % 100));
}


/* make the disk look busy. */
disk()  {
int n,i;
long l;
    for (i= 2; i--;)  {
         n= open("foo",0);
         for (l= 1000L; l > 0L; l--);
         if (n != -1) close(n);
    }
}
```

```
                         *    *    *
/* Randomly choose a DOS message */
dosmsg() {
int i;

    i= rnd % 10;
    switch (i)  {

        case 0: cprintf("Eh? I wasnt paying attention \r\n");
            break;
        case 1: cprintf("invalid directory\r\n"); break;
        case 2: cprintf("Insufficient disk space\r\n"); break;
        case 3: cprintf("Do you hear music?\r\n"); break;
        case 4: cprintf("Invalid number of parameters \r\n");
            break;
        case 5: cprintf("File not found or I lost it\r\n");
            break;
        case 6: cprintf("I see no FILES here\r\n"); break;
        case 7: cprintf("Nothing happens\r\n"); break;
        case 8: cprintf("Insufficient memory\r\n"); break;
        case 9: cprintf("Error creating file or pipe\r\n");
            break;
        default: printf("rnd = %d default?\r\n",i); break;
    }
}

/* "execute" a command */

command()  {
    disk(); disk(); disk();
    cprintf("Bad commmmmmand or file name\r\n");
}
```

MORE BIG LAUGHS

☐ "WHERE'S THE KIDS, HERMAN?" by Jim Unger.   (157958—$2.25)

☐ "APART FROM A LITTLE DAMPNESS, HERMAN, HOW'S EVERYTHING ELSE?"
   by Jim Unger.   (163435—$2.50)

☐ "ANY OTHER COMPLAINTS, HERMAN?" by Jim Unger. (136322—$1.95)

☐ "NOW WHAT ARE YOU UP TO, HERMAN?" by Jim Unger. (156323—$2.50)

☐ "THE CAT'S GOT YOUR TEETH AGAIN, HERMAN" by Jim Unger.
                                                (160517—$2.50)

☐ "FEELING RUN DOWN AGAIN, HERMAN?" by Jim Unger. (156374—$2.50)

Prices slightly higher in Canada

Buy them at your local bookstore or use this convenient coupon for ordering.

NEW AMERICAN LIBRARY
P.O. Box 999, Bergenfield, New Jersey 07621

Please send me the books I have checked above. I am enclosing $_____
(please add $1.00 to this order to cover postage and handling). Send check or money
order—no cash or C.O.D.'s. Prices and numbers are subject to change without
notice.

Name_____

Address_____

City _____ State _____ Zip Code _____
Allow 4-6 weeks for delivery.
This offer, prices and numbers are subject to change without notice.

FIND THE ANSWERS!

☐ **101 BEST MAGIC TRICKS by Guy Frederick.** Top magician Guy Frederick lets you into the inner circle of those who know what others never can even guess about how magic really works. Includes handkerchief tricks, card tricks, mind reading tricks, and much much more! (158598—$3.95)

☐ **THE COMPLETE BOOK OF MAGIC AND WITCHCRAFT by Kathryn Paulsen.** The unique guide to everything you need to know to become a witch— with all the ancient and modern recipes, spells, and incantations essential for magic, witchcraft and sorcery.   (168321—$4.95)

☐ **WEDDINGS: A COMPLETE GUIDE TO ALL RELIGIOUS AND INTERFAITH MARRIAGE SERVICES by Abraham J. Klausner.** The Essential Handbook for every couple planning a wedding or renewal vows. "A significant work!"—S. Burtner Ulrich, Rector, St. John's Episcopal Church, Yonkers, N.Y.   (153898—$3.95)

☐ **HOW TO BUY A CAR FOR ROCK-BOTTOM PRICE by Dr. Leslie R. Sachs.** Get the lowdown from the man who went undercover as a car salesman to learn the tricks of the trade. What you don't know about buying a car could cost you thousands.   (149610—$3.95)

☐ **HOW TO KNOW THE BIRDS by Roger Tory Peterson.** Here is an authoritative, on-the-spot guide to help you recognize instantly most American birds on sight. Includes a 24-page color supplement. (129393—$4.50)

☐ **THE AMATEUR MAGICIAN'S HANDBOOK by Henry Hay.** Fourth revised edition. A professional magician teaches you hundreds of the tricks of his trade in this unsurpassed, illustrated guide.   (155025—$4.95)

Prices slightly higher in Canada

Buy them at your local bookstore or use this convenient coupon for ordering.

NEW AMERICAN LIBRARY
P.O. Box 999, Bergenfield, New Jersey 07621

Please send me the books I have checked above. I am enclosing $_____
(please add $1.00 to this order to cover postage and handling). Send check or money order—no cash or C.O.D.'s. Prices and numbers are subject to change without notice.

Name_____

Address_____

City _____ State _____ Zip Code _____
Allow 4-6 weeks for delivery.
This offer, prices and numbers are subject to change without notice.

There's an epidemic with 27 million victims. And no visible symptoms.

It's an epidemic of people who can't read.

Believe it or not, 27 million Americans are functionally illiterate, about one adult in five.

The solution to this problem is you... when you join the fight against illiteracy. So call the Coalition for Literacy at toll-free **1-800-228-8813** and volunteer.

Volunteer Against Illiteracy. The only degree you need is a degree of caring.